PENGUIN BOOKS

Binge Trading

At the age of nineteen, Seth Freedman ditched his university place to take a job at a City of London stockbrokers. It was 1999, the height of the dot-com boom, and within months he was handling millions of pounds' worth of client orders. He dealt for Swiss banks, spending time in Geneva learning to trade bonds, before leaving to take his client base to another London brokerage. On growing disillusioned with the life he was leading in the City, he moved to Israel and spent fifteen months in a combat unit of the IDF – where he grew even more disillusioned, albeit for vastly different reasons. He has written for the *Guardian* about the financial markets and the Israeli–Palestinian conflict. He is the author of *Can I Bring My Own Gun?*.

D0207952

Binge Trading

The Real Inside Story of Cash, Cocaine and Corruption in the City

SETH FREEDMAN

PENGUIN BOOKS

PENGUIN BOOKS

Published by the Penguin Group
Penguin Books Ltd, 80 Strand, London WC2R ORL, England
Penguin Group (USA) Inc., 375 Hudson Street, New York, New York 10014, USA
Penguin Group (Canada), 90 Eglinton Avenue East, Suite 700, Toronto, Ontario, Canada M4P 2Y3 (a
division of Pearson Penguin Canada Inc.)
Penguin Ireland, 25 St Stephen's Green, Dublin 2, Ireland (a division of Penguin Books Ltd)
Penguin Group (Australia), 250 Camberwell Road, Camberwell, Victoria 3124, Australia
(a division of Pearson Australia Group Pty Ltd)
Penguin Books India Pvt Ltd, 11 Community Centre, Panchsheel Park, New Delhi – 110 017, India
Penguin Group (NZ), 67 Apollo Drive, Rosedale, North Shore 0632,
New Zealand (a division of Pearson New Zealand Ltd)
Penguin Books (South Africa) (Pty) Ltd, 24 Sturdee Avenue,
Rosebank, Johannesburg 2196, South Africa

Penguin Books Ltd, Registered Offices: 80 Strand, London WC2R ORL, England

www.penguin.com

First published 2009
1

The moral right of the author has been asserted
Set in 12/14pt Bembo
Typeset by Palimpsest Book Production Limited, Grangemouth, Stirlingshire
Printed in England by Clays Ltd, St Ives plc

ISBN: 978-0-141-04364-7

www.greenpenguin.co.uk

Penguin Books is committed to a sustainable future
for our business, our readers and our planet.
The book in your hands is made from paper
certified by the Forest Stewardship Council.

To Evil

Contents

Prologue: 'Fuck That, They're Bust!'

The last day of March turned out to be a bountiful beginning to spring, thanks to the inept management team of Stern Group. A manufacturing business with a rapidly deteriorating reputation, it had for years been a target of bear raiders – stock market speculators who tried to drive its share price downwards. Stern Group now appeared to be in its death throes, yet there were still the foolhardy – and just plain foolish – out there who were keeping the share price propped up by throwing good money after bad and buying more stock.

The fatal blow seemed to have been struck one morning in March 2004, when the company put out an announcement saying that it had uncovered a hole in its accounts. That was a clear signal to sell the shares, regardless of the price that they were trading at after the statement.

If, as the news seemed to imply, they were on the way to going bust, then the Stern shares ought to be worthless. That meant any price above zero was a price worth shorting at (selling stock we didn't own, in the hope we could buy it back for delivery at a cheaper price later on). The shares had halved immediately on the announcement – but because the news had broken before the market opened, it hadn't been possible to open a short the second that the news got out. This would put many traders off dealing, believing that the 50 per cent collapse meant that the shares wouldn't go any lower. But, after a brief chat with my client, we stuck to our guns and piled in.

I sold a million Stern shares at five pence to start with, because, with the price bouncing up and down like the proverbial whore's drawers, I had to be cautious. I planned that we'd add to the position when the dust had settled a bit. The trade started to look a bit weak when the stock began to get hoovered up by the mug punters convinced it was due a recovery – and Michael, my boss on the trading floor, started getting on my case about it.

'Well you'd better make sure the client's got the cash to cover it if this goes pear-shaped,' he snapped, always nervous of the customer's cavalier attitude to trades going against him. Michael played things straight: investing clients' money for the long term, in sensible ways with sensible strategies. He hated my clients' day-trading way of doing things, as well as their complete lack of caution when they dealt.

Two minutes after calming Michael down, I started getting jumpy as well, though I managed to put on a brave face all the while.

'It's just a dead-cat bounce,' I said to my client. 'They'll settle down, I promise you.' But the price was telling a different story. Huge volume, and the shares were climbing steadily – trades were now going through at five and three-quarters pence, then six, then a couple even printed at six and a half.

We broke the golden rule and decided to double up on a bad trade.

I sold another million shares at six and a quarter pence each, meaning that we were now exposed to the tune of over 110 grand in a stock that refused to dance to our tune.

'If they hit eight pence or higher, I'm calling in the trade,' warned Michael, who was breathing down my neck as though he was some kind of fucking customs official.

'Shut up, Mike,' I replied, not prepared to be talked to like a three-year-old just because he didn't like the way the wind was blowing.

Just as he started yelling at me again, my screen froze, and the trades stopped printing. In place of the price was now a yellow S – the shares had been suspended pending a further announcement, according to the Reuters newswire scrolling past the bottom of my monitor. For my part, it was a relief that the rot had stopped for now – if they were suspended, at least they couldn't go any higher, and the short position couldn't get any worse.

It was make-or-break time, I realized, as I took the lift to ground, shakily lighting a cigarette and smoking it nervously all the way down to the tip. Just because I believed the company was terminally wounded meant nothing if the next announcement they came out with was good news. Even though the respite may only have been temporary for Stern Group, the price would still go through the roof, thanks to the bears scrambling to cover their shorts, as well as all the bargain hunters piling in for a quick trade on the up-side.

I felt sick. If the company said anything positive – anything at all, even 'the hole in the accounts is bad, but not as bad as we'd feared' – then the shares could be twelve or thirteen pence within seconds, and we'd be down well over 100 grand.

Too tense to go back to the desk, I paced furiously up and down the alley as I waited for the moment of truth. As I walked around like a condemned man, a call on my mobile from Dave confirmed my worst fears – with a frightened voice, he blurted out, 'They're printing at twelve and a quarter . . .', prompting my chest to tighten violently. But, before I could reply, he collapsed in a fit of laughter. 'Fuck that,' he cried, 'they're bust!', sending me reeling from panic to joy in two seconds flat.

'Wanker,' I shouted, half-heartedly trying to muster some anger at his stupid joke. 'What are you winding me up for? Fucking buy back the short – go and pick up the winnings.'

I raced back inside and read the announcement for myself. Stern Group was dead and buried, though the shares were still suspended. Getting one of our seasoned dealers on the case, Dave told him to make inquiries round the market about how cheaply he could pick up a million Stern. He found the stock on offer at two and a half pence in an off-market deal, and my client didn't need asking twice. We closed out immediately, leaving him ninety grand better off, less the handsome commission being charged on the trade.

I was more than happy with that little coup, especially given how viciously wrong it had been going just minutes earlier. Once the market shut on the stroke of half four, it was off to score some coke and toast another fortuitous deliverance from the jaws of defeat.

Like a greyhound hurtling out of the starting cage, I dashed straight to Kentish Town to pick up from Sammy, telling him breathlessly on the phone to bring fourteen grams of the white stuff, which was music to his ears as well as to my salivating gums. Deal done, I raced home in a cab to survey my loot. Piled up on the dressing table, this was a beautiful score, and was only even vaguely acceptable because I'd convinced myself that this was a final fling before I called time on the City and relocated to the Middle East.

Thus began a seventy-two-hour marathon that took me to the brink and back – and all under the ironic banner of liberation from the powder.

Introduction: The Siren Call of the City

To trade for a living is to continually take giant leaps into the unknown. You live at the mercy of markets that behave like bucking broncos at the best of times, and out of control rollercoasters at worst.

The trade requires courage, arrogance, self-belief and nerves in equal measure. No matter how many pints or grams you imbibed the night before, irrespective of how many furious rows you've been having with your girlfriend, regardless of how disastrously wrong your last deal turned out – the minute you hit the buy button and go live, the only thing that matters is stacking up profits. Letting yourself become assailed with doubt to the point that it clouds your judgement and saps your confidence is a deadly sin: once your belief in your own abilities departs you, there is no way back.

Imagine another person, fund or company placing hard cash in your hand – and giving you free rein to trade it. It's like being injected with a drug as strong as anything you can buy over (or under) the counter. Your client is trusting you to take care of their money in the same way as a frantic parent hands their sick child over to a surgeon in an operating theatre. While they pace nervously up and down the hospital halls, you are not permitted any such luxury – the account lives or dies by your hands, and you are tasked with playing God as you make split-second decisions over what to do next.

The longer you've been in the game, the more superhuman you begin to feel: once you're used to donning your cape and flying round the marketplace every day, the sensation of self-assurance becomes second nature, and your personality begins to be moulded around the macho image you portray during trading sessions. Yet while the heady cocktail of egocentric qualities can bring extraordinary success, they can also cause spectacular falls from grace, engulfing not just the trader involved, but his firm, the shareholders and even the entire global financial system – as was shown so devastatingly throughout 2008.

The year saw several dramatic cases of individuals crashing and burning: young Parisian trader Jerome Kerviel was SocGen's answer to Nick Leeson, and then came alleged Ponzi-scheme shyster Bernard Madoff. But the entire financial industry was rocked by across-the-board examples of staggering over-confidence and dearth of regulation. Investment banks toppled like dominoes, exposing time and again the lackadaisical attitude of traders and management alike towards risk.

Firm after firm has been forced to admit that their Icarus-emulating traders had sailed too close to the subprime sun. When their wings burned, their exploits dragged the rest of the economy (including millions of investors and savers) down with them. The fallout from the crisis continues to have knock-on effects which threaten to shake capitalism to its foundations. Yet while there is a consensus forming that traders and bankers need reining in – for the good of the world at large – there is very little that the layman knows or understands about the inner workings of the market, and the mindset of those bidding and offering billions of pounds' worth of shares every day.

I lived and breathed the stock market for six years, jettisoning my place at university in favour of diving head-first into a world of high living, hard drugs and even harder cash. I joined the City in 1999 as the dot-com boom was en route to its spectacular crescendo — when shares doubled, tripled, and quadrupled in price at the blink of an eye. There was no end in sight to the fortunes to be made.

After rapidly rising from the lowly ranks of back-office post-boy to partners' assistant in the heart of the dealing room, I passed my SFA (Securities and Futures Authority) exams and began trading for a burgeoning list of my own clients. Our firm dealt for some of the biggest names in both the financial and high-society spheres, and I soon became as at ease running through the state of the market with lords and ladies as I was scoring coke from East End wideboys round the back of Mile End station. Within months I was comfortable with trading seven-figure CFDs by day and racking up lines by night. The market felt like the most natural of environments in which to unleash my inner beast.

However, as the years passed and the alarm bells began ringing, it was clear that the longer I continued in such a financially rewarding but spiritually bankrupt atmosphere, the closer I'd inch to the point of no return. I didn't want to turn forty with only my cash for company, having eschewed all my other dreams in order to turn financial tricks for a living. That some brokers, dealers and traders never quite get over their youthful excesses was exactly the reason I got out when I did. I was still in my tender twenties, and the world was still my oyster — especially with the financial clout that my spell in pinstripes now afforded me.

So I left, swapping Hermès ties and Armani suits for an M16 and army boots. As part of my immigration to

Israel I spent fifteen months in a combat unit of the IDF (the Israeli army), putting as much distance between myself and my coke-fuelled City days as I could and playing my part in the defence of my adopted country. Upon demobbing, I found myself at odds with the Israeli system that I had embraced only a year or so earlier. The combination of sobering experiences policing the illegal occupation of the West Bank and an urge to assist those seeking to challenge the status quo led me to begin writing political commentary about the Israeli–Palestinian conflict. But I never took my eye off the City.

Despite taking the money and running in my midtwenties, I am painfully aware of the magnetic pull the market exerts. When the credit crisis burst on to television screens and newspaper front pages in 2008, my latent passion for trading surged to the forefront of my mind. I began gambling on the FTSE, reacquainted myself with my ex-workmates in the City and was commissioned to write a series of articles for the *Guardian* on the state of the stock market. My pieces kicked up a storm among outraged readers, many of whose values rested on a bedrock of leftist principles and who were affronted at the City-philic attitude I displayed in my writing.

The more stick I received for daring to suggest that it wasn't simply the City that was to blame for the culture of instant-credit, instant-returns infusing society, the more I realized how important it was to shine a spotlight on those working within the Square Mile's borders. Just as I had made it my mission to challenge the misconceptions about Palestinian society, attempting to give voice to those living behind the concrete slabs of Israel's security wall, so too I believed that the City's residents deserved a fair chance to speak out.

In this prolonged winter of discontent it's easy to accuse the world of high finance. But the truth is much stranger than the fiction propagated in the national press. One such example of the way in which media scape-goating seeped its way into law during the crisis was the cavalier fashion in which short-selling (selling stocks the trader doesn't own in the expectation that they can be bought back cheaper later on) was deemed to be the root of all evil, with anyone engaging in the practice being labelled an enemy of the state.

In typically knee-jerk, crowd-pleasing fashion, the SEC (American financial regulator) announced a toughening-up of the rules regarding 'naked short-selling' of US securities – a move that was inevitably followed by the British regulator. The practice was cited as having exacerbated the slump in global stock markets, with Lehman Brothers' CEO Dick Fuld apparently threatening to rip the arms off those shorting his com-pany's stock and sending its share price crashing through the floor.

Shorting has acquired a reputation as the demonic twin of 'going long' on shares in the hope that they will rise in price. But, as Fuld well knows, there is nothing illicit about the technique. There is no fundamental dif-ference between going long or short, since both types of trade are financed on assets being lent: either money or stock. Shorting involves borrowing shares until the set-tlement period has expired, at which point the shares must be returned; going long involves borrowing money to pay for the shares, which is only repayable at the end of the agreed timeframe. Given their parity, and given that the stock market is heavily driven by the whims of those buying and selling, if someone decides that the share price of a company is about to fall they have as much right to act on that impulse as anyone anticipating a sudden rise.

The SEC, Fuld and even the British Chancellor, Alistair Darling, scapegoated short-sellers purely to deflect attention from their own failure to contain the financial hurricane. When there was a major bull market, none of them were complaining that 'naked long' positions were driving the market higher.

During the dot-com boom of the late nineties, the years of so-called 'irrational exuberance', share prices regularly went through the roof over the course of a few hours' trading. While the going was good, the regulators smiled benignly down upon the market players. Restrictions on client borrowing were relaxed, and customers were encouraged to use margin to take out far larger positions and thus increase brokers' commission rates.

Anyone caught short during the wild surges of the dot-com years was in danger of losing all their money and more, thanks to the huge downside risk in shorting shares. Despite their losses, they had no one to blame but themselves; it was they who called the market wrong, and they who had to pay the price when the time came to settle their debts.

Now, however, there was the absurd demand being made in some quarters that people long of stock – those who had lost out during this prolonged bear market – should lay the blame at the feet of their savvier peers who bet the other way. Because that's all trading boils down to: making bets on the direction of share prices, index values, oil futures and any other tradable commodity. As in the world of bookmaking, so in the stock market: for every backer, there is someone out there laying the price. If there wasn't, there wouldn't be a market at all.

Simon Cawkwell, the most famous short-seller in the City, for whom I acted as broker during the second half of my market career, mounts a scathing attack on the regulators.

'[The rules] are infantile; they are the emotional reaction of children,' he says mockingly. 'They [will] have no effect on the market whatsoever, since they have nothing to do with real life at all. They are a raft of propositions offered by very silly fools to even sillier fools.'

Warming to his theme, he suggests that disgruntled investors and taxpayers swivel the barrels of their guns away from the City, and towards Westminster.

'The problem is not short selling', he assures me. 'The problem is the electorate who voted in a socialist [Gordon Brown] who thought he could run the economy. He talked about "prudent stability" just to [ensure he became] prime minister. He's a fucking nuisance.'

Cawkwell's ire was understandable, given that the regulators' anti-shorting overtures threaten the foundations upon which his business was based. Darling's comment that he was 'extremely anxious that we avoid a situation where people can manipulate markets, causing huge harm that is totally unjustified' was calculated to unite hordes of embittered investors in a witchhunt against their undeserving peers.

The bottom line was that had the heads of the banking behemoths and their watchdog counterparts exerted more control over the extent of firms' exposure to high-risk debt, there wouldn't have been this degree of bear market (from which short-sellers could profit) in the first place. That no one saw it coming is a tragedy – for employees, shareholders and everyone else caught up in the crisis – but to set up straw men in their desperate attempts to play the blame game is disingenuous.

Bear raiders like Cawkwell are as vulnerable to the risks they take as any other investor. They are entitled to make their money in the best way they know how and to milk as much out of the markets as they can, based on the strength of their instinct and nouse. To deny them that opportunity, based on spurious reasoning and political opportunism, is shutting the door of the stable five along from the one out of which the horse actually bolted.

Action such as the SEC took, rather than calming the jitters running through the market, actually threatened its stability. But that didn't stop them doing it all the same, since in the credit-crisis climate of fear and loathing, any points that could be scored at all were worth their weight in gold (though perhaps not at current prices).

The FSA had their pound of flesh as well: short-selling in financial stocks was banned shortly after the SEC's move to outlaw the practice. Ostensibly put in place to prevent market abuse, the crackdown was applauded by many commentators in the perverse belief that the only reason world indices were plummeting so sharply was thanks to those traders shorting into a falling market.

A month later, and it was clear that they were wrong. The SEC had already lifted their draconian ban on shorting financial shares, which lasted for three weeks and had no effect on halting the slide in US markets. The S&P index lost 21.5 per cent of its value during the period of the ban, and the embargo was viewed by market experts as actually increasing volatility in the indices as a result – hardly a desired side-effect of their prescriptive measure. The FTSE collapsed in similarly spectacular fashion during the same timeframe; a prediction that was widely made by those clued-up enough to spot the short-selling ban for what it was. In January 2009 the UK's Financial Services Authority (FSA) bowed to the inevitable and lifted its own ban on shorting financial stocks.

The fiasco over short-selling, in tandem with a myriad of uninformed opinions espoused during the sub-prime aftermath, further convinced me that the City must first be understood before it can be judged – and that includes getting to know the people who work at every level within its structure. In writing *Binge Trading* my mission is to delve behind the incendiary headlines and firebrand political rhetoric, and discover what life in today's City is really like.

The credit crunch was in full flow when I flew back to London and returned to my old Square Mile stamping ground in late autumn 2008. Fear coursed not only through the veins of the tens of thousands of workers within the financial sector, but also those of millions of other Britons, watching as the crisis deepened with every passing day.

Uncertainty paralysed the collective consciousness: banks refused to lend money to one another (let alone businesses and homebuyers), share prices plummeted like lemmings from a cliff, market goliaths were brought to their knees by burgeoning debts and insufficient capital. At one point it appeared that the entire global financial system was on the verge of collapse.

Against such a harrowing backdrop, talking to the traders and bankers at the centre of the crisis was not easy: many would speak only on condition of anonymity, and even then with a defiance or defensiveness. Others appeared stunned at the swiftness with which their whole world was unravelling, staggered that the foundations upon which their careers and lives had rested for decades were now trembling violently in the fierce winds that howled around the City. Many wore the hangdog expressions of severely hung-over revellers – the 'morning after' effect bringing them crashing down to earth after years spent partying in (what had seemed) a never-ending bull market.

My research took me back on a journey through the Square Mile, meeting brokers, dealers and even psychoanalysts. But most of all I got up close with the traders: the men and women staking millions of pounds on shares every second of every trading day. My position as a former broker gave me access to areas off limits to outsiders, allowing me to delve into the psyches of those with whom I spoke and understand what drives them to do what they do.

Simon Cawkwell points out in one of his books that 'gamblers frequently experienced, or think that they experienced, absolute authority in childhood' – an observation which sits well with the personalities of many of the traders I interviewed. While many market participants entered the profession in blinkered fashion – following other members of their family, or lacking inspiration about other careers – once in, there is a common sense of growing wedded to the cause.

The stock market is a powerful toxicant, rewiring many traders' systems and reshaping their personas to fit the model of egotistical gamblers. And not just by day – the trappings of wealth combined with that omnipotent feeling led to some of the most extreme hedonistic activities, both as a way of letting off steam and announcing to peers that the individual concerned had made it big.

But in some ways my and my friends' after-hours activities were no different from those of our non-City peers. While other eighteen-year-olds were skipping lectures at university, those of us who turned our backs on higher education to go chasing the money down the gold-paved streets of the Square Mile were playing out our own acts of teenage rebellion. The difference was that, with money in our pockets and the world at our feet, there was no reason to call time on the adventures. Many came perilously close to the edge – and plenty of individuals and firms did find themselves plunging over the edge of the cliff.

As the City crashed and burned in 2008, it was clear that the rest of Britain would be dragged down with it. The financial sector accounts for over 10 per cent of the UK's GDP, and is the capital's largest employer, accounting for the jobs of around 1.3 million Londoners. The knock-on effects of the credit crunch caused panic in both the press and political arenas, with City scapegoating becoming the order of the day. Fury emerged towards the perceived culprits for the crisis.

However, in the rush to apportion blame, the hypo–crisy of those pointing the fingers blinded them to the reality of the situation. London's financial hub, the heart that pumps blood through every artery of the British economy, is populated by people no better or worse than the rest of the nation's citizens. Yes, they've made mis-takes of mammoth proportions in their handling of the latest round of boom and bust, but then so have many others benefiting from the bubble of recent years.

Rising house prices, cheap credit, consumer durables, cheap holidays when the pound was strong: all added to the sense of invincibility which infected both the City and the wider echelons of the public. The boom was a collective delusion.

As well as trying to dispel some myths about stock-market culture, I also wanted to write about my own experiences – the massive deals, the larger-than-life characters, what it actually feels like to trade, how swiftly drugs and alcohol can envelop those on the City scene, and so on. Much of my own account is contained in the first chapter, but I have also added my insights throughout the rest of the book. I hope that my first-hand knowledge of the market's machinations adds another layer to the story, enabling me to draw out the stories of market players and comment from the vantage point of a former insider. Where I refer to my own experiences as a trader I have changed the names of all my former colleagues to protect their identities, as well as the details of specific trades and dealing patterns.

After summarizing my own experiences in the market, *Binge Trading* then leaps straight into the subjects of my research, with a study of their own market beginnings: why they entered the profession, what attracted them to the market and how they adapted to the high-octane environment of the City – an arena which doesn't suffer fools gladly, nor cuts newcomers any slack.

The next chapter, 'The Long and Short of It', explores what traders actually do for a living. It's not good enough to treat traders as one homogeneous mass, carrying out deals in the same way as punters at their local bookies. Via first-hand explanations of their daily business, and detailing the plethora of skills and traits required to handle such high-pressure business, those with millions at their fingertips speak frankly about life on the City frontline.

The corruption endemic to certain parts of the financial system is explored in the next chapter, '"One for the Boys"'. One broker blows the lid on the alarming practices he witnessed, detailing how easily false rumours can be spread, how confidential news is shared ahead of release, and how trading profits can be siphoned off. If you're punting on shares from outside the City, you'll always be a step behind the insider dealers.

Next I tackle the myths that surround the Square Mile. Tales of rampant cocaine abuse in dealing rooms make for good copy but do little to paint a true picture of life on a trading floor. From first-hand experience I know only too well that drugs are not happy bedfellows with trading. The idea that billions are being wagered on the markets by fired-up fiends with shaking hands and dilated pupils just doesn't wash – and in this chapter I explain why, as well as dispelling other myths about City boys and their lifestyles.

In the next chapter, the current form of the stock market is set against the backdrop of modern society. There's an exclusive interview with a trader at the centre of the sub-prime crisis, who details how the wheels came off the speeding train and why. Other City figures pour out their hearts about how uncomfortable working in the market has made them, whilst at the same time explaining why they feel unable to call time on their careers and walk away (relatively) unscathed.

There's a whole section devoted to the extraordinary figure of Simon Cawkwell, who made his name by exposing Robert Maxwell's empire as being no more than a house of cards. He allows me to watch him at work, as he spends his days trading the markets and gambling on football and racing with equal dedication – living up to his reputation as one of the City's most feared bear raiders and savviest punters. After this glimpse into Cawkwell's world, I look into the darker side of the City – what happens when all goes spectacularly wrong, and what the ramifications are for those involved, as well as those who entrusted them with their fortunes.

Finally, I ask traders and bankers for their views on the future of the markets, given the latest round of collapsing indices and mass lay-off of workers in the financial sector. I discuss with them whether the public could – and should – be convinced to trust the City once more, and what measures ought to be put in place to ensure disasters such as the sub-prime collapse are prevented from happening again.

A little knowledge is an incredibly dangerous weapon in the hands of the wrong people. If this book can shine at least a touch more light on the day-to-day machinations of the Square Mile, and into the minds of those who operate its complex machinery, then I will have done my part.

1. I Was a Teenage Trader

The first indicator that a life in the City was on the cards came at an interview for a private school in north London. I was eight. Asked by the headmaster what I wanted to be when I grew up, and not having been prepped by either my parents or primary school teachers, I opted for the truth. 'I want to be an estate agent,' I replied, unaware that my response was out of line with the standard wished-for career paths of doctor or lawyer.

'Why on earth would you want to do that?' he replied, his face a combination of amazement and world-weariness.

'Because that's what my uncle does,' I explained, 'and all he has to do to make £5,000 is pick up the phone.' I wasn't lying: it was the post-Big Bang eighties, and my uncle's Mayfair property dealership was well placed to perform such financial sorcery on a daily basis.

Ten years later, and I was living my dream, albeit selling stocks and shares rather than bricks and mortar. It started with a three-month spell of work experience in a private-client City brokerage during my gap year, arranged via my grandfather's friendship with the firm's chief executive, which put paid to any vague desires I had to go to university. Living in Manchester reading Modern Middle Eastern History had initially seemed a tolerable way to delay getting a real job, but that was before I'd opened the door to a parallel universe.

On my first day of work experience, I was still in the

dark as to all this. Not to mention what the stock market actually did. All I knew was that for each week spent stuffing envelopes in a stoned haze I would be two hundred and fifty pounds richer. The suit and tie was a drawback, but no deterrent to my first faltering footsteps into the brave new world.

The first thing that struck me was the sheer opulence of the Square Mile. Emerging blinking into the light at Moorgate Station, I was blown away by the shimmering surfaces in every direction and air of pristine smartness about everyone. Poppy-red Ferraris vied for space with sleek, chauffeur-driven Bentleys at every set of lights, or so it seemed to me at the time, the previous night's skunk and a starry-eyed dazzlement combining to paint the City as a cash-rich theme park of paradisical proportions. The realization that it was more like Dante's Inferno than Paradise wouldn't come until much later.

I slunk along in the shadows that first morning, cowed somewhat by the air of complete authority with which my City co-residents stalked the streets, and bemused as to how to make the instant shift from sixth-form stoner to suave City boy. Fortunately I was put to work deep in the bowels of the building, three floors down from the dealing room, ensconced in airless quarters with two Essex boys and a couple of other members of the non-broking flotsam, whose role was simply to do the unseen bidding of the trading-floor titans above.

My first morning was spent trying to decipher the thick Brentwood accents of the duo with whom I shared an outsized square desk, failing miserably at my task. The loudest was Ricky, a brash boy not much older than myself. He took me under his cockney wing from the off, schooling me in what (he thought) was the unwritten City code necessary for survival in these shark-infested waters.

'Look 'em all in the eye when you're talking to the brokers,' he told me defiantly. 'They were all like you once. They got fucked over by their bosses, and now they're gonna love doing the same to you, so just lay back and take it like a man, even if it hurts – and it will.'

Ricky's life lessons were interrupted at regular intervals by tales of what he would, could or should do to the various blondes whose paths crossed his. There was nothing for me to do but listen in a state of faux-impressed silence; there was no work to speak of for me to carry out, save for nodding deferentially whenever one of the brokers ventured past us on their way to smoke at the back of the building.

At that early juncture there was absolutely no reason either to curtail my heavy weed smoking or to emerge from my self-imposed shell of silence, since there was no one of any note worth impressing, nor any effort required more mentally taxing than holding my tongue as Ricky drawled endlessly on about his libidinous prowess.

I was given a brief, perfunctory tour of the dealing room on my first afternoon, in the company of a bored-looking, middle-rank broker who had been granted the dubious honour of being both assistant to the partners and head of the firm's team of juniors. His schizophrenic role meant that he switched painfully between being the little people's best friend when no one else was around to adopting a stance of snarling, sneering ball-breaker as soon as one of the top dogs came into sight.

He quickly filled in the gaping holes left by Ricky and his sidekick, bringing me up to speed within a few minutes about what went on in the dealing room, why it happened at all and where I fitted into the food chain. He turned all of Ricky's advice on its head, advising me against any form of bolshevik standing up to the bosses, although he concurred with Ricky's assessment that, come what may, I had to lie back and think of England rather than dispute any punitive actions against me.

Stepping on to the dealing-room floor for the first time, I felt as though I was running the gauntlet without so much as a pocket knife for protection. I tried to make myself look small and sober, my skunk-saturated mind convinced all eyes were on me. Of course no one paid me the blindest bit of notice: they were far too concerned about the state of their clients' trades and their own commission figures to give a damn about the latest underling off the production line.

I didn't register on radar until we got to Cyril, the boss of the firm, who bared his teeth like a Bengal tiger upon being told who I was. I'd got the job thanks to his friendship with my grandfather, but that meant little now that I was alone in Cyril's private jungle.

'You're here to work,' he told me sharply, 'and you're not to let me or your grandfather down, understand? That means looking smart, acting smarter, doing everything you're told, regardless of who's telling you to do it, and above all remembering exactly who you're working for.'

He didn't need to tell me twice; all the signs pointed to him ruling the firm with an iron fist, and from the tales to which I'd already been privy, the less I saw and heard of him, the better. It would be two years before he was facing off to me and threatening blue murder in front of a desk full of brokers. For now he had better things with which to occupy his time.

The stock market remained a mystery to me during my

first few weeks. I immersed myself in filling envelopes and Rizla, neither knowing nor caring what went on around me. Gradually, however, the realization dawned on me that the City was dripping with cash, and anyone standing under the right branch could get soaked themselves.

My first encounter with what I considered to be the big time was a clandestine chat with Simon, a stockbroker-head-of-juniors hybrid, who cottoned on to my bloodshot eyes and figured I could help him and the others with a bit of off-market dealing. 'One of the partners wants to score a bit of blow,' he told me off-handedly during a cigarette break one afternoon, 'and it'd look good for you if it's you that picks it up for him.' After going through a pantomime of acting coy, and Simon telling me not to be so 'fucking cagey' and to stop worrying about being caught out, I grabbed the two fifties he was proffering in my direction, promising to get as much as I could and deliver the goods the next day.

I only scored an eighth of an ounce for him, loathe to carry more than that with me into work, given the heady aroma that even a few joints' worth gave off. I marked it up by a fiver and prepared to hand back the seventy pounds change once I saw Simon downstairs. Slipping it to him before the market opened, I then went to hand back the remaining cash. 'Keep it, Seth,' he purred, thrilled at our below-the-counter transaction and knowing – quite rightly – that I would be in his pocket from now on.

It wasn't the size of my unofficial pay cheque which hooked me, but the casualness with which I'd been paid off. I had friends dealing weed at universities all over England, making just enough here and there to support their own fume-filled habits, but here I was in a world where cash rained down like manna from heaven. I and my mates had always been chided by our parents for our laissez-faire attitude to money; now I was doing a deal with a bloke in his thirties and he just didn't care. Once I started climbing the ladder and seeing for myself how the bulk of the brokers operated, I realized they all lived in Never-Never Land. I wanted to be knee-deep in it with the rest of them.

My timing was perfect, likewise my chameleon-esque skills at adapting swiftly to new situations. The dot-com bubble was starting to inflate, and – after ingratiating myself with Simon and the partner with a penchant for weed – I became more and more of a presence on the dealing-room floor. I was tasked with menial duties such as fetching the partners' coffees, or handing out their contract notes at the end of the day, allowing me to make the acquaintance of the more friendly faces on the desks and see what went on in the heart of the operation. I began reading about the market at home and on the Tube, not quite knowing why and how it all happened, but finding myself seduced by the culture all the same.

By this point, I was on the verge of going to Israel for a hedonism-fuelled six months of debauchery – a final fling all the kids in my community enjoyed before embarking on their university adventures the following year. I was still thinking I'd be joining my friends at Manchester, but the seeds of doubt had been sown in my mind, and what was germinating was a feeling that perhaps the City was a blessed alternative to mind-numbing study in some cold provincial backwater.

By the time I was midway through my sojourn in Israel, I was hoping for a return to another Holy Land: the one at the end of the Northern Line rainbow where I'd spent the preceding three months. One afternoon, my mind struggling to cope with the after-effects of yet another ecstasy-and-vodka binge in downtown Jerusalem, a call from my parents hammered the final nail into my undergraduate coffin. 'Simon just rang. They want you to go back to the firm to work in the dealing room,' my mum said.

I didn't need telling twice. Once I'd backed out of my university place, all my attention turned to the City. The rest of my extended spring break with my fellow revellers played itself out via a heady mixture of hard drinking and even harder drugs, before I found myself back on terra firma, decked out in my City finery and raring to make a go of the chance I'd been given.

My parents had decided to buy me a flat up the road from their house – 'if you're going to work, you might as well have a mortgage and play the part properly,' they asserted, instantly transforming me into a home-owning member of the London workforce, to my untrammelled delight. It was 1999, I was nineteen, suited and booted, and more than up for the challenge.

With the technology boom in full flow, the firm's corporate finance department was inundated with new companies wanting to ride the internet wave and list on the market. All this extra work meant many more hands were needed on deck in the junior department. A few new faces were brought in and I – by virtue of being the only one who had even the slightest clue how the dealing room operated – was put in charge of our little team. All of us were urged to take the relevant exams as soon as possible, so we could start trading for clients in our own right. I made it my mission to be the first to make the leap from junior to broker, and suddenly I was propelled from a dogsbody doing menial tasks to the lofty position of partners' assistant, taking over Simon's duties whilst he went on to bigger and better things.

Keith was my overall boss and tormentor for the time I spent working for the partners. He ran the Swiss side of the business, dealing for various private banks and individuals in Geneva and Zurich, and he took his role seriously. I spent all day hunched over my Reuters terminal, watching minutely every move of the FTSE stocks for him, under strict instructions to alert him whenever a share price got close to the limits flagged by his ever-demanding clients.

It was a baptism of fire; I was flailing around with no one to turn to for help. Keith had learned his trade under the harsh tutelage of Cyril himself and believed in the 'spare the rod, spoil the child' school of thought when it came to dragging me up by the bootstraps. Resistance was futile, and within weeks I was firmly under his thumb, where I was doomed to stay for the best part of two years.

My world became defined by the shimmering lights on the trading screens. Hundreds of stocks flashed their rise and fall across the screens, with the Reuters news bar spewing out company announcements like a Gatling gun. My eyes were trained to follow every flicker. Banks of phone lines were available at the push of a button, two handsets per man – one for the right hand, one for the left – thoughtfully built of toughened plastic to withstand the phone-to-wall smashing that took place whenever a deal fell through.

We sat in long, straight rows in the trading room, like slaves chained in the hold of a Roman galley. Our chains were gilded ones, granted, but they shackled us all the same: from 7 a.m. till 4.30 p.m., five days a week, we barely left our desks. I was an extension of Keith's eyes and ears, trained to work for my master like a hyped-up guide dog. There were six screens shared between each pair of traders, the monitors stacked on top of one another in a tight semicircle.

Only one woman had permeated the unofficial men-only barrier set up around the dealing room, and she didn't hang around long in the end. Otherwise, the entire floor was populated by men. The well-dressed, well-connected north London boys were groomed to become the next generation of brokers, skilled at flattering the clients. The Essex boys who joined the profession ended up as dealers, equally obsequious, penetrating the inner circle of the market to get the best prices buying or selling shares. We brokers advised our clients and kept them up to speed on their investments, then – once we'd been given orders to complete for our customers – we took the trades to the dealers, who used their contacts in the marketplace to get us the optimum prices for our clients.

The relationship between brokers and dealers was a symbiotic one, though below the surface there was little love lost. The brokers looked down on the uncouth mannerisms of the barrow-boy dealers, who in turn mocked the slickness of their cufflink-sporting counterparts. For my part, I yearned to be a rough and ready dealer, out getting hammered with the other market-makers every lunchtime. But – in the caste system that was the stock market – I was doomed to remain on the broking side of the divide.

By virtue of my position on the partners' desk, I was able to sip from their font of wisdom, which, whilst at times shallow in terms of their skills at analysing companies, more than made up for it in terms of the depth of their client-handling skills and charm. It became apparent early on that those for whom they dealt were, in the main, amongst the upper echelons of British society in terms of their wealth and saw their trading activity as little more than a pastime, a more socially acceptable form of gambling than backing horses all day at their local bookies.

At that point, I was being swiftly schooled in talking to the clients on my boss's behalf, keeping them sweet if he was otherwise engaged, reading them their price lists and taking any orders they wanted executed on their accounts. I found myself conversing with House of Lords peers, members of the landed gentry, minor celebrities and captains of industry, all of whom required little more than a healthy dose of ego massaging, followed by a quick rundown on the state of the market, both of which I was more than willing to supply now that I'd lost my dealing-room cherry and was becoming more and more proficient in the not-so-noble art of sycophantic salesmanship.

The internet-led market mayhem was now in full swing: what had begun as a murmur now became an intense, daily roar. Prices in hitherto unknown small-cap minnows were doubling, tripling, even quadrupling in price on a daily basis, and the general consensus amongst brokers and clients alike was 'fill your boots'. They did, in droves – the brokers dealing on their own accounts as well as their clients', more often than not, since the opportunity to take advantage of the surging market seemed far too good to miss.

'All you fuckers who wanna get on, get on; all you fuckers who wanna get off, get off,' was Keith's bizarre mating call whenever he spotted a trade attractive enough for him and the other partners to get involved in; bizarre, because the lion's share of the time he was the epitome of suave, sugared refinement, until the excitement got too great and he morphed temporarily into pseudo-Essex mode.

I and the other juniors wanted in on the act, opening our own accounts and aping our lords and masters with our own smaller personal deals. It made scant difference what stocks were being bought: we only saw the companies in terms of the percentage returns we could make. Invariably we juniors cashed out too early, too skittish to hold our nerve and wait for the really serious moves. The partners all performed trading alchemy on a regular basis, making five- or sometimes six-figure profits after perfectly timing their in-and-out dealing.

Cash was cascading down on investors like the Niagara Falls by then. There was a stampede by would-be clients, hungry to get involved. I was encouraged to study for my SFA exams, being promised the moon if I knuckled down and got myself qualified to deal for my own client base, which the firm would supply.

For the first time in years, I stopped my weed consumption; not even the spectre of GCSEs or A-levels had had that effect, but I had my eyes firmly on the prize this time. I came, saw and conquered the exam in one fell swoop; more thanks to the stunning simplicity of the material I had to study rather than any application on my part. The veneer of stockbroking was just that, I realized: a smoke and mirrors act, with the qualifications no harder in truth than the theory section of a driving test.

Passing the exam first time marked me out as someone with a bright future in the business; since there was no grading system, the way of determining one's prowess was much more binary. I was taken more seriously from then on; almost immediately I was building up my own client list, at first from the scraps that the partners tossed my way. Not that I cared; the thrill of advising clients, and having them deal on my suggestions, transformed me into a cartoon superhero in my own fevered mind.

Here I was, still only nineteen, advising clients with million-pound portfolios by day, whilst by night I couldn't see further than the blazing cherry at the end of my joint or my latest fumbling, teenage conquests.

The mismatch between my professional and private life came to a head after my first face-to-face client meeting, the build-up to which shot my nerves to pieces. A client for whom I'd been dealing over the phone had carved out time in his diary and was coming up to London just to meet me. He had several accounts, for various members of his family, and was the polar opposite of the trading, punting clients with whom I felt far more at home. He had asked me to identify several long-term investment opportunities for his funds, seeking low-risk, high-yield stocks that would sit nicely alongside his ultra-safe, gilt-edged treasury holdings and – ideally – not cause him even the faintest of sleepless nights.

I rose to the challenge by brazenly stealing ideas from the Merrill Lynch analysts' reports to which we had access through some back-door arrangement. I had no idea why they were promoting Shell, Diageo or any of the other shares they rated strong buys, but I made my pitch like a true expert. Sitting across from him in one of our sleek oak-and-chrome meeting rooms, I held his gaze and waxed lyrical about healthy dividend payments, strength of balance sheets, upside potential and all the other catchphrases I'd absorbed by osmosis having spent so long sitting at the feet of my superiors on the partners' desk upstairs.

My client lapped it up, placing a series of substantial orders there and then, before asking me if there were any slightly racier, non-FTSE100 stocks I would be buying for a shorter-term move. Freezing up for the first time in our meeting, I racked my brains and came up with the model-train maker Hornby – more out of deference to my childhood reminiscences than any knowledge of the stock's performance. I spun a good yarn about the growth of model enthusiasts in Middle England, harked back to my own experiences sending OO-HO trains around the track in my bedroom, and he was more than happy to spend a few thousand following my advice. That he banked 20 per cent on the stock a month or two later was all luck and no judgement on my part, but it did wonders for my confidence and (often misplaced) belief in my own trading instinct.

The immediate outcome of our meeting was more sobering, and should have set alarm bells pealing. Thanks to the success of my salesmanship, I'd earned over a thousand pounds in commission fees for half an hour's work – a huge sum to someone in his first-day-at-school shoes.

To celebrate it seemed only right to toast my new-found earning power in time-honoured City fashion; namely, to go out, score a quarter ounce of coke and let the good times roll. The client meeting had been on a Friday; by Saturday night I was sitting in my flat with my mates, chomping my jaw like Red Rum at the starting post, talking nineteen to the dozen, insides frozen all the way from my gums to half-way down my throat. I had hit the big-time, or so it seemed in my self-adoring state. But I was to come crashing back to earth with a deafening thud.

By the time Monday morning rolled around, I was coiled in the foetal position in what I assumed were my death throes. I'd not eaten for two days, and when I forced myself out of bed I stood on shaky, foal-like legs, button-ing up my Burberry trenchcoat against the howling wind and stumbling blindly in the direction of the station. By the time I made it to my desk, I looked like the living dead, and even the usually tyrannical Keith softened after one glance at my haggard visage. Murmuring about a heavy dose of the flu, I assured him I would struggle on, but he told me to take myself home. I didn't need asking twice; the screens were literally swimming in front of my eyes, and there was no way on earth I'd be in any fit state to field calls or deal for clients by the time the market opened. I dragged myself home and made a pact with myself to knock the hard living on the head.

After seven days of home comforts and nothing stronger than a Marlboro Light, I was firing on all cylinders again and spent the next twelve months clean as a whistle. That period coincided with an upsurge in my broking business, thanks to a fruitful relationship with two unashamedly short-term trading clients. One of the more professional partners had tried to teach me the finer art of analysing company accounts, believing – correctly – that it was an area of expertise sorely lacking in my arsenal.

When I proved resistant to his entreaties to pay attention to balance sheets, he gave up, instead passing me an account of his that had lain dormant for the best part of a year, telling me, 'He's your type of punter – you'll be two peas in a pod if you get it going properly.' Prophetic words: after a fortuitous first trade, in which I advised the client into a stock all the partners were buying, and took an overnight 13 per cent profit, we moved on to bolder things, taking huge positions on FTSE stocks at will with barely a nod at the merits (or lack thereof) of the underlying companies.

My client loved to punt, along with his business partner, who had a lucrative sideline as a professional poker player.

Their love of short-term trading was more than matched by my eagerness to wade into the market and stake six-figure sums on big-ticket trades, and we ran hand-in-hand up the share-lined avenues of T10 trading. T10 meant buying stock on ten-day delivery, so the client didn't have to pay for the shares up front, and would ideally close out the position for a profit before deadline, meaning no cash ever had to be laid out. T10 has now largely been usurped by Contracts for Difference (CFDs), at least in the larger company sector, but then it was the ideal way for clients to take leveraged positions with only a fraction of the would-be requisite cash in their accounts.

I had to balance my new-found position as broker in my own right, managing a burgeoning customer base of potentially risky clients, with my original role as Pinocchio to Keith's overarching Geppetto. Inevitably my dual roles were never going to sit comfortably, and I railed against Keith's authority with the petulance of a pubescent teenager. Things came to a head on more than one occasion, when Keith found me too busy servicing my own clients to back him up on the Swiss desk. When trouble came calling Keith called Cyril, who came storming down from his office on high to the dealing floor to dish out punishment to his bolshie sub-subordinate.

His threats went in one ear and out the other for the most part, but it was clear that I was going to have to make a choice between performing verbal fellatio for my clients on a daily basis or for Keith's. There was no argument in my mind: if I was going to turn trading tricks for a living, I'd far rather make a broker's cut of the commission than live off the minuscule percentage Keith handed to me from his sirloin cut of the firm's earnings.

In the interim, however, a relapse into the all-night,

all-encompassing world of coke sped up the process of my protracted divorce from the firm – and it was all Keith's fault. Had he let me have a Monday morning off to recover from a wedding in Paris on the Sunday night, rather than force me to stay up round the clock, catch a red-eye Eurostar and be back at my desk for 7 a.m. sharp, then I wouldn't have been forced to take the grown-up's ProPlus to tide me over – not just that night, but for the next three long years . . .

At the start of the summer of 2001 I was marching further away from my roots, blinded by this world where money talked and cokeheads talked louder. It was becoming apparent, from my dealings with fellow brokers and traders, at pubs, clubs and opulent parties in the West End, that coke was as much a status symbol to be proudly sported as a house in St Johns Wood or a new soft-top DB7.

Since I already owned bricks and mortar, I could divert my funds to more ostentatious, and ultimately frivolous, pursuits: hitting the rails of Nicole Farhi, Dior and Armani on weekends, dining out every night in the bistros of St Johns Wood and Marylebone and generally doing my damnedest to play the part of the cash-rich, spiritually overdrawn twenty-year-old I now was. I kept my original two-bedroom residence, buying a four-bedroom flat in an art-deco building up the road, which I moved into, along with three friends who rented rooms from me.

At work, I was still the partners' lapdog, but enjoying the same luxuries as them thanks to my semi-privileged position on their desk. Every day we placed our orders with the in-house chef, and our lunches would be deliv-ered to our desk on fine china plates with silver service;

we were treated like Premier League footballers: every whim catered to, every need pre-empted.

We got taken care of by clients and companies alike; freebies were bobbing round in the bucket waiting to be hooked like ducks at a fairground. For example, our relationship with Mean Fiddler got me backstage VIP tickets to Glastonbury for me and three friends, whilst the rest of our peers traipsed round in the mud with the paying public. (That schism had become apparent a year earlier as well, during the May Day riots when protestors attacked City institutions: many of my friends, as well as my sister, were in the thick of it on the side of the demonstrators, while I was ensconced in the dealing room, watching events unfold on the plasma screens above our desks.)

As part of Keith's efforts to wean me off my trading clients and back under his wing, I was shown the earthly delights of Geneva, first when we hosted a lavish party for our clients, and later for a two-week spell working in our bond-dealing office near the lake. On the occasion of the party, I flew out to join Keith, Simon and Cyril himself, getting a taste for the refined high life that Swiss bankers enjoy. Things were going swimmingly until, on the plane home, I opted to remove my tie – leading to a barrage of abuse from Cyril, who asserted that, as an ambassador of his firm, I had to eat, breathe, copulate and sleep with a Hermès tie hanging noose-like from my throat.

I'd been invited to the wedding of the sister of one of the other juniors, a beautiful French girl for whom, after she became my flatmate, I'd found a job at our firm. The wedding took place on a Sunday afternoon in the Jewish quarter of Paris, before moving on to a château in the countryside, where the revelling went on long into the night. I didn't look back until I was covered in sweat on the Eurostar home, heart racing. What hadn't killed me had certainly made me stronger, though: I appeared to be made of stronger stuff than the last time I'd wed my septum and coke in holy matrimony, and once I got back to my desk, I made it through the working day with barely a whimper.

So I'd unlocked the gates of Cocaine Towers, and I could see myself becoming a permanent resident. I forged a friendship with my new dealer, a loaded, Knightsbridge-dwelling financier with a Masters in International Banking. He sold, I bought, we went out drinking together and became mates. Meanwhile, I noticed that my sleeping habits had changed. I used to sleep at night. I didn't any more. For cocaine was a jealous god; if I was going to get on it, I had to give up all activities that got in the way – and sleep was the first to go.

Which is fine if you're pulling an all-nighter on a Saturday and living sensibly the rest of the week. But when the call of the powder leads you to do it once or twice during the week, and soon every night, then you're in trouble. However, trouble to a young stockbroker is not the same trouble that a mechanic or bus driver might get into: money was no object, no barrier to my love of the good times.

If it had been, I might have been unable to continue the hedonism at this pace. Either way, two more elements were abruptly added to the factors governing my future, in the form of the duo of planes that took down the World Trade Center one sleepy lunchtime in September. It began as any other day in the market; the brokers reclining regally in their seats, swapping tall tales and winding each other up. 'The Queen Mother's died,' was the

favoured rumour of one loud-mouthed partner at the
other end of the desk. He switched story all of a sudden,
telling us, 'Plane hits World Trade Center' in a voice that
suggested he was reading it from the Bloomberg news
ticker. Most people thought this was another ruse, but we
switched channel to Fox News and saw the live images.

I called my trading clients to let them know the news,
then was midway through filling my dad in on the story
when a second plane came hurtling out of the heavens
and into the adjacent tower. 'Hold on, Dad, I think
they're just showing a rerun . . .' I began, before my brain
computed what I was witnessing, at the same moment
that thousands of other traders cottoned on to the new,
awful reality.

Pandemonium ensued. The dealing room was filled
with manic traders, all preaching a Doomsday scenario
and selling at will. The sky was falling in, on the markets
at least, and our dealers were deluged under a barrage of
sell orders. These came both from brokers closing out
positions and those opening up new shorts, in order to
capitalize on what would clearly be an index collapse of
mammoth proportions. The afternoon played out in a
whirlwind of frenzied trading activity, until Stock
Exchange bosses called early time on proceedings, heed-
ing the advice to evacuate the City and Canary Wharf in
case a copycat attack was on the cards for London.

While the rest of the capital had downed tools, those
on the trading floors that day had serious work to do:
money was being haemorrhaged from long-only funds,
and at the same time those with the ability to short realized the potential if they got on and sold the fuck out of
the market. Rightly or wrongly traders are trained – and
paid – to react to news, good or bad, so there was no

time like the present to get in or out of whatever positions they saw fit.

In the aftermath of 9/11 the markets went into a prolonged downturn. At that point I was fighting with my superiors and our compliance staff, who were growing ever more concerned about the size of the trading positions I was running for my clients, believing I shouldn't have been allowed that much autonomy. When things finally came to a head, in part sparked by my refusal to rein in my clients – who always were good for the money in the end – and in part by my falling asleep at my desk after another all-nighter, my bosses and I decided to part ways for good.

Both parties had had more than enough, so I resigned and was free to take my clients elsewhere. Which was all well and good, but I had the little matter of three months' semi-paid leave to attend to first, and already I could feel the money burning a hole in my septum.

What followed was a ninety-day spell of seriously depraved behaviour. I loved it at the time, but looking back this was rock bottom. I was free, I was going out with one of my flatmates – a gorgeous blonde down in London to pursue an acting career – and I was doing whatever the fuck I liked, most of which was coke.

I was only twenty-one and already had half a million pounds' worth of property, so I felt no remorse about the stupid amounts I was spending on drugs. I treated it as no more than a mini-gap year, the lull before the next trading storm. Time stood still whilst my heart raced furiously, spurred on by the chemicals coursing through my bloodstream.

Life was an endless loop of drink, drugs, Domino's, clubs, computer games, and causing my girlfriend no end of stress, until finally the time came to don the pinstripes once more. I'd hammered it in a fashion that I never would again; the hangover was deservedly vicious.

I found I'd suddenly turned a corner in my career path. Despite an inauspicious start at my new brokerage – during which I refused to fully give up my bad habits and knuckle down to any real work – once I got going properly, I was starting to look and act like a far more grown-up version of my previous incarnation. It all began with a casual inquiry by my new desk partner, Nick, who pointed to a Bloomberg screen and asked me, 'So, what do you think of BP's graph, then?' Costing upwards of £3,000 a month, Bloomberg is an all-inclusive system providing live prices, market data, stock graphs and charting tools for every index, every currency, every commodity on the planet. A phenomenal piece of equipment, if you know how to use it – and Nick certainly did.

For my part, I'd been schooled in the Reuters trading system, which was equally powerful, but I'd barely scratched the surface of its wealth of data. I'd relied thus far on tips from my bosses, mixed with a healthy dosage of both wings and prayers, in my trading decisions, a state of affairs that was clearly utterly unacceptable to my new dealing room co-residents. 'It looks pretty ...' I replied, as Nick waited. My next word never came, as the sum total of my ability to read the graph he was showing me was simply that the coloured lines looked pretty.

So began the short, sharp, shock treatment at the hands of Nick and our boss, Michael. At first it was like something out of the Topsy and Tim children's book series: Topsy and Tim analyse Fibonacci charts; Topsy and Tim discuss support and resistance levels; Topsy and Tim look for currency-play ideas. It seemed embarrassing at first but it was also an incredibly liberating experience. While I still understood only a fraction of what they were telling me, it stood me in better stead than the three years at my first firm. However, my formative years on the partners' desk had by no means been in vain – I'd learned the art of salesmanship, I'd built up a good list of contacts both in and outside the market, and most importantly I'd gained a lifetime of workplace confidence in comparison to my friends still labouring away at universities.

I balanced my daytime trading and my nocturnal hedonism for the best part of two and a half years in my new surroundings; at times precariously, but falling in love with the physical and mental acrobatics of the trading screens. If you put me in front of a Reuters, Bloomberg or SETS screen now, I'd be straight back into the groove – fingers flying lightly over the keyboard, calling up charts and data at will, the pathways through the system still second nature. You never forget, like you never forget how to ride a bike or load an M16 (depending on preference). The sheer thrill of getting an order, punching it into the computer and watching your trade hit either the bid or offer on the screen was what did it for me: the fact that this was live, this was dangerous, this was a video game being played out in real life, and it made me feel alive.

CFDs were all the rage, and my clients and I gladly stepped up to the plate, using the facility to take even bigger and braver positions than before. One set of clients decided to make Vodafone their stock of choice, eschewing all other trades in favour of the market megalith that was Voda, trading it day in, day out, with varying degrees of success. Vodafone's size meant it attracted an enormous trading volume, allowing traders and punters to elicit decent turns out of its daily movement thanks to the sheer number of similar deals being carried out on the order book. A 1 per cent return was magnified into 5 per cent in real terms, if the leveraging was on a scale of five times the underlying cash position, which did wonders for both their returns and my commission figures. At 0.2 per cent per trade, I could take £800 commission out of a ten-minute-long, 200-grand punt, and I gleefully banked my winnings.

Whilst I still serviced my other clients, the real thrill for me was in the big-ticket, short-term trading; nothing (legal) made me feel as fired-up as when I was executing and monitoring a FTSE CFD on behalf of my biggest clients. I was hunched over the screens, eyes flicking from news bar to share price to index level and back again in a flash; just like I used to for Keith, but this time entirely for the benefit of my clients and, ultimately, me.

Along with my new-found penchant for the brasher side of the market came my ascent to the next level of high living. The drugs were the same, but the setting for their ingestion changed; I was now being driven round in clients' roofless Bentley Continentals and F1 Spyders when they came to visit me in the City. We'd dine at Michelin-starred restaurants, moving on to the Sanderson Bar or the West End clubs their friends owned.

Expenses were no issue as long as the clients were doing the business – and they were, in spades. My best clients did five figures of commission a month by themselves, so spending a thousand pounds on a Cristal- and coke-themed lunch didn't raise any eyebrows (outside of the gents' toilets, that is). A typical day out with them would last the best part of fifteen hours, see us refuel at least three times from a dealer who was more than happy to chase us round town, dropping off shrink-wrapped supplies, and drench ourselves in alcohol until only the dawn chorus forced us to what was left of our senses and off to our respective homes.

Back at work there was an air of respectability and efficiency. I was required to attend pre-market meetings round a boardroom table at seven o'clock every morning, when the agency brokers presented their stock ideas for the day ahead (as I struggled with how to knot my tie and do up my shoelaces). The firm was split into three parts: a hedge fund, an inter-dealer brokerage and then us, the private client broking division. There was no reason to stray into one another's terrain save for occasional cross-border trades or casual chats.

Nick, one of the best teachers I'd come across during my short time in the City, was moved over to the hedge fund, killing off an almost brotherly relationship between the two of us. I'd spent more time with him on a daily basis than with my friends, family or girlfriend, knowing his every idiosyncrasy and turn of phrase. It was the same for anyone on dealing-room floors: your world was whatever and whoever was within touching distance of your seat: one man either side of you, those sitting across the desk from you behind the banks of screens, and the effervescent market itself, bubbling over in liquid-crystal clarity as it bared its soul to you from the opening bell until close.

Nick's departure coincided with a wave of ennui that swept over me. Much as I still was turned on by the action of the markets, and the fast living that the money I was earning allowed me to enjoy, an early seven-year itch was starting. I was caught in an endless loop, one which could ultimately lead to my downfall – whether from an obsession with the market at the expense of all else, or via off-market self-destruction. I went to work, made money, spent it on drink, drugs and other pursuits, struggled into work again the next day . . . with no more nourishment for the soul than the occasional film, book or play.

I wanted for nothing, but the idea of turning round at forty and the sum total of my achievements having been the amount of money I'd stacked up chilled me to the core. Plenty of my bosses and peers had that mindset, and from what I could tell the acquisition of yet more wealth had done nothing to bring them happiness or anything like true satisfaction. The process of removing myself from the markets didn't happen overnight; nor did my overhaul of my self-centred, self-serving value system take place in a revelatory Damascene moment. There was plenty of time for that; in the interim, I pushed doubts to the back of my mind and carried on tearing childlike round the adventure playground that is the City.

On one self-indulgent night, I briefly gave up on any plans to leave the Square Mile, believing I had it all, and fuck the yearning that occasionally gnawed away at the far reaches of my consciousness. Sitting on the roof terrace of Coq D'Argent, five floors above Bank Station, a receptionist from another firm on my lap, a nose full of coke and a throat coated with glass after glass of sixteen-year-old Lagavulin, I looked up at the sky and silently offered thanks for such fortune. I was sitting prettier than I'd ever imagined when I first stumbled dazedly down Moorgate all those years before. As I kissed the girl astride me, I felt complete in a way that I hadn't for years.

The next morning, after reality kicked in and the two gashes inside my nostrils began seeping blood, the joy of the night before seemed a distant memory. The knowledge that even that pure pleasure hadn't lasted longer than the effects of the powder meant I was more than ready to call it a day.

My discretionary trading was starting to become more of a penance than a pleasure; likewise had my control over my non-discretionary clients' activities. I'd had run-ins with clients, thanks to the calibre and character of those for whom I was dealing – men who'd lash out in a rage when the chips were down and try to get me fired, then smile sweetly the next day and carry on as if nothing had happened – so I had no qualms about turning my back on them. Similarly, much as I'd loved working with Nick, Michael and one or two others, I'd come across ten sharks for every true friend I'd made in the City, and I myself was in danger of becoming one of the people I despised.

The basest instincts come to the fore when the name of the game is money, and your standing in society is based purely on how much you've made and how fast you've made it. I was as guilty as the next man of adopting this skewed outlook – but it wasn't until I left it all behind me that I realized how deeply I'd been bitten by the lust for lucre. When I was trading millions on behalf of my bosses and clients, I saw nothing amiss about spending £500 on a Cavalli sweater or a grand on a drug-fuelled night out. Cash that could be made in an instant could be spent the same way, and there was always more where the last wad came from.

In the end, I got out because it was clear to me that it was a case of now or never. Spending all day with men in their late thirties who couldn't see past the next deal, the next line of coke or Porsche Carrera set alarm bells ringing – if I didn't want to turn out like them, I had to call it a day. Much as the casino atmosphere was limitless, fast-paced excitement for a boy in his mid-twenties, as a long-term lifestyle choice it was shallow. It wasn't worth selling my soul.

Ultimately, trading is as addictive a pastime as any other form of gambling, and as any drug. It becomes a way of life – a way to define yourself, to convince yourself you are the centre of the world and believe you are all-powerful in the grander scheme of things.

Hitting a button and effecting a seven-figure trans-action is the stuff of fantasy for most people in the real world, but when you've been doing it every day since you were nineteen, you soon lose your sense of reality and get swept away in the carnival atmosphere. Sipping a quiet pint in the pub after an adrenaline-packed day riding the market rollercoaster doesn't quite sate the appetite, so heavy drinking, hard drugs and all the other trappings of overindulgence soon become standard fare.

But the plight of the trading addicts is masked by their clothes, jewels, cash and 'success' – few question their happiness, since they seem to have it all. These aren't junkies huddled under railway arches begging for loose change, but their entrapment is no less acute – quitting is as hard for a trader as it is for a heroin fiend. I don't say this in an attempt to solicit sympathy for the devil – I've got none myself, and don't seek to pull the wool over anyone's eyes when it comes to how they view the City and its darker traits.

What I refuse to do, however, is single out those within the confines of the City as in some way a different, more destructive breed of human being. With this book, I aim

to bring to light the stories of a variety of City players
– traders, dealers, brokers, market makers and hedge-
fund managers – in order to show that they are products
of both a system that uses them for its own devices and
a society that allows this to happen without a murmur
when everyone's getting a slice of the action.

I lived and breathed the City for six years, gliding
along to what would have been an easy, cash-rich career
for life, except that I pulled the emergency cord and
disembarked. After the research for this book, I am hap-
pier than ever that I jumped. Because life in the City is
by no means the bed of roses that it's painted to be. What
goes up, comes down; whether on the graphs of a
Bloomberg screen or in harsh, 3D, Technicolor reality.

2. Born to Trade

Sitting in the lounge of his spacious west London house, children's toys strewn across the parquet floor, Daniel Barnes (not his real name) is reminiscing on his own childhood games.

'I enjoyed counting coins when I was a baby,' he remembers, a smile playing across his lips as he conjures images of himself almost thirty years ago. 'Even my own kid loves putting coins into our little plastic Ferrari. It's just one of those things I always enjoyed, running around the house, looking in every corner, in the drawers, in my dad's pockets, for any coins and then coming to him and saying, "Look, I have eighty pence."'

His path from pre-school bean-counter to postgraduate financier at a bulge-bracket investment bank was pre-destined, he believes. Despite reading Philosophy at Oxford, he never took his eyes off the prize: making money.

'Some people love having the money, and that's what drives them,' he explains. 'For me, it's actually making the money – the end product in itself is neither here nor there, really. I have much more satisfaction putting my competitive streak into practice, losing, winning and experiencing those emotions, rather than just having the end product handed to me on a plate.'

For that reason, if he was to inherit £100 million tomorrow, he wouldn't call time on his money-making pursuits; rather, he'd simply 'trade with it, or use it for something else where I can apply my competitive streak'.

Barnes's career has spanned several major banking institutions, culminating in his playing a significant role in structuring and selling CDOs, the three-letter acronym that has become a four-letter word since the subprime bubble burst and the credit crisis hit home around the world. He was part of a four-man team making millions of dollars in fees for his firm every time they assembled a new product and put it out on the open market. However, his beginnings were far humbler.

'When I was sixteen or seventeen, I thought, yeah, I'd love to be a trader,' he recalls. 'I used to go to the bookies, I used to bet and think, this is great, you just put money down and you either make big or you lose, but you take it as it comes. So during university I got myself the internships, I went on trading floors, I read books like *Market Wizards* about trading psychology. The thrill of making money – the thrill of seeing a zero by your name, or a zero in your bank accounts, suddenly shoot up – is an incredibly good feeling. I don't have a very expensive lifestyle – I live in a nice house and whatever else, but I don't go out splashing the cash.'

His entry into the City was carefully calculated to maximize his earning potential in the shortest space of time, in line with his shrewd analysis of what makes the markets tick.

'It isn't always about just profitability; it is about perception, playing the system, and making sure that you have good sponsors in the right place,' he says. 'Because, when it comes to bonuses, it's not just [based on] how much money you have made. If you deserve to be paid a million dollars, it's because someone else will be willing to pay you a million dollars, maybe more, so they've got to pay you just enough to keep you. That's the way that I always looked at it . . . from a very monetary perspective.'

Barnes is by no means alone when it comes to his reasons for diving head-first into the heady world of high finance. Rarely have I come across anyone who gravitated towards the City out of inherent love for the machinations of the market or an ambition to rewrite the rules. Merely playing the game and reaping the rewards on offer is enough of a pull for most. The Sirenesque call of the Square Mile is seductive, particularly when you've grown up in a society where, as Barnes puts it, 'success happens to be gauged by money'. This is an age where celebrities and sportsmen are deities – worshipped in the *Sunday Times* Rich List and the glossy pages of *Hello!*. Even the witch hunt against the City during the credit crisis is infused with a healthy dose of jealousy. No scapegoating feature on 'greedy' bankers is complete without a rundown of individuals' salaries and the playthings they have amassed.

Against this backdrop, it is hardly surprising that many of those seeking validation will alight at the City. It also has a veneer of respectability about it, which enables those fuelled by monetary desires to be admired, rather than admonished, by those around them. Had Barnes discovered a latent prowess for backing horses or predicting football results and made the local Ladbrokes his place of work, it is far less likely that he would have found acceptance from his nearest and dearest. There are more similarities than differences between the worlds of gambling and City trading, but the two are miles apart in terms of social status. The City remains the place where the paths of pure lust for lucre and yearning for social standing collide. This ensures each fresh financial intake is cut from identical cloth.

Paul O'Connor (not his real name), a retired sales trader at one of the European banking goliaths, makes no bones about the catalyst that propelled him City-wards in his teens.

'I joined the City in 87/88 – boom time, Thatcherism – and I saw how much money could be made pretty quickly. At my interview I was told that in three years' time I could be earning £100,000 and, being seventeen and naive, I bought into it. I bought into the idea that I could have money and then prove that I was better than anyone else.'

Yet when talking about his twenty-year City career he utters not a single word of praise for the markets; instead he views it as a means to an end, namely to pursue the acting life he always wanted.

'I did want to go to drama school when I was eighteen, but I was too scared. I thought I had to get money behind me first,' he recalls. 'I was addicted to wanting to prove myself, and quite materially driven. I was driven by money, but I wouldn't say I was addicted to money itself. [It was more about] my working-class background, and probably my sexuality: I wanted to prove myself as good as other people, and that's why I became addicted to making money.'

The flickering screens of a trading room can entrap wide-eyed youths from all walks of life, be they aristocracy, well-off middle-class kids, or those from harsher beginnings. The City appears as no more than a salubrious set of slot machines to those whose only experience of the world of finance is screaming headlines about fortunes won, lost and won again by traders and fund managers staking billions of pounds.

Steven Gold (not his real name), an investment manager looking after over £60 million of client funds on an advisory basis, recalls similar feelings as he took his first faltering steps in the market.

'It was just really exciting. All my friends were doing these really boring jobs as trainee lawyers and the like, while I was watching people trading $50 million of Reuters shares. I was just out of university and I'd never seen a number that big.'

Others follow their fathers into the trading fray. Michael Parnes is son of Anthony 'The Animal' Parnes, one of the most colourful figures of the yuppie-led eighties boom.

'My father has always been quite a character and a prolific stockbroker,' he says. 'I remember growing up not really understanding what the stock market was, or what my father did – all I saw was that he was very well respected, had some powerful people around him and was at the peak of his career. I enjoyed listening to him on the phone – he was always on one phone, if not four at the same time – he looked busy and successful, so from a young age I identified whatever he did as success-ful. It was in the blood. I was drawn to it.'

This moth-to-a-flame effect is not confined to the offspring of traders and brokers but greatly enhances the attraction to those with familial connections – if only because of the exposure to the City and all its trappings at an early age. Darren Carver (not his real name) quit school before completing his A-levels, following in his father's footsteps.

'He was a stockbroker on the market floor, so that was always the back-up plan. I had a City grounding. I'd come up there a couple of times as a child during school holi-days and seen a bit, and in between taking my O-levels and A-levels I did a bit of work as a messenger for a City firm, and some back-office work in the summer holidays. I went back to school for six weeks, and [it compared badly to] having a few quid in my pocket.'

Dr Harry Freedman, chief executive of London careers consultancy Career Energy, draws distinctions between City job-seekers based on their backgrounds.

'There are two sorts of people that go into the City,' he observes. 'One is the people who go in as traders, [they] very often can be from working-class backgrounds: they have a bit of energy, a bit of oomph, and they want to make some money. But the main group of people going into the City are driven by family pressures or the sense that they have to have a proper career. Rather like people who become lawyers at the age of twenty, they do it because they don't want to have just any old job; they've got to have a job that gives them security and respectability, and the City's one of those places where they get that.'

According to Dr Freedman, those from the latter camp allow their craving for both financial and social standing to damp down their creative urges – preferring to simply do the bidding of their new masters, whatever the side-effects of such submissive behaviour.

'I think you can take this all the way back to school,' he says. 'You've got the sort of teenagers who put their lives and their personalities first and follow their hearts, and you've got those who put their respectability and their conventionalism first, and they follow the career path. That's the same whether they're swotting for exams or whether they're going to go into a profession or into the City. They're the ones who will be prepared to bully and be bullied in the City, because it's the price you pay for this great big salary, for this nice car, and so on.'

The culture of bullying was what first alerted me to the darker side of the Square Mile, having witnessed it from the very start of my career. The hierarchical structure of the dealing room, combined with the almost entirely male environment in which it existed, meant the worst public-school posturing and power-wielding flourished. The weak were preyed upon by those seeking to establish themselves as alpha figures, and this behaviour was actively promoted by bosses who saw it as a sign that the perpetrators were displaying all the skills needed to survive in the City jungle.

As the head of our team of juniors, I was ordered to use my position to keep in line those below me in the pecking order, despite the fact that they were my friends, and that I was barely above them in the wider scheme of things. When the partners wanted someone to go and get their coffee, the order would be routed through me, and I would have to select one of the other juniors to head off to the shop for them. If they didn't come back quickly enough, I was told to call their mobile phone and reprimand them for their tardiness. If I protested, I was told, 'It's either them or you – we gave you the order, so it's your responsibility.' I witnessed the same behaviour throughout my time in the Israeli army, but at least then there was a sense that a failure to follow commanders' instructions could put lives in danger, rather than simply lower the temperature of a broker's cappuccino by a couple of degrees.

Of course, to those dishing out the punishments, there was rhyme and reason to their actions, along the lines of 'if I can't trust you with an order for a coffee, then how can I trust you to execute million-pound trades?' Steven Gold expresses no bitterness about his initiation, asserting that his completion of menial tasks was key to moving up the ranks.

'I came in on day one and I didn't have a clue – the first two or three months were unbelievable. I just didn't know what was going on. People talking a different language. You may just be getting sandwiches for everyone, but then you realized they are testing you. If you say no, it's a blot on your character, whereas if you get an order for twenty sandwiches right, it is noted.'

Being left in the dark as to the actual trading taking place meant Gold felt 'a bit left out of it in the beginning. I was a spare part. People would talk to me only when they had nothing else to do.' So he struck up friendships with the back-office guys.

'I used to go out drinking with them. I wouldn't think anything of going out Friday lunchtime for three hours, having a load of beer and coming back to the office. A lot of the dealers were drinking. One died at my first firm: he just blacked out and died. He was only in his thirties.'

The rewiring of a straight-off-the-boat junior in the City does not extend simply to the setting up of money as an idol; the whole lifestyle must be embraced. Darren Carver 'fully embraced' the culture of hard living, thanks in part to his acceptance that it was a case of 'horses for courses'.

'You're naturally attracted to a certain sort of crowd, and I was attracted to the drinking culture. You've got to imagine at seventeen, eighteen or nineteen a broker's going to be taking you out – I was making markets to begin with – and when you've got a broker taking you out at that age, you're not earning massive money, but you haven't got to stick your hand in your pocket all night . . . everyone was doing it, you know? Everyone.'

Part of the reason behind the propensity to socialize in the pubs and bars of the Square Mile is the need to make new contacts and put out feelers for business, Carver says. He joined the markets just after the Stock Exchange floor made way for the computerized trading system, which put even more pressure on brokers and dealers to spend their free time keeping up appearances in the right watering holes.

'I can imagine the floor was like a big club, and then people went to work in offices, so you had to maintain relationships with brokers,' Carver explains. 'I think a lot of the time it was disguised as a means for getting business, but [at the same time] you did develop relationships.'

Having to show aptitude not just for trading and client handling but also for the murkier side of the business meant that anyone who stood out for the wrong reasons was at an immediate disadvantage, as Paul O'Connor found to his cost.

'There is definitely a "one of the boys" mentality, that if you're seen as being onside then you're going to get on more. It's an issue that I had, being gay. I didn't socialize as much as colleagues; I didn't join in the Monday conversations of "who did you shag on the weekend?" I wasn't out; I felt like it would harm my career – so I just kept myself to myself. I definitely felt on the back foot, because the guys that were getting involved in the whoring and the drinking were more onside with the bosses. I wasn't given access to certain clients, because those clients were given to the blokes of my age who could take them out and show them a good time.'

At the other end of the scale is Jeremy Lyon, who took to the markets like a fish to water. He was not motivated by solely monetary factors, but rather by the way of life. He began in a bygone age, in the late sixties, when the Stock Exchange was simpler than today.

'I had an uncle who was in the market already and I lived with him,' he recalls, eyes shining. 'He was a stock-broker, dealing with gilts and bonds, and he introduced me to a partner at Pinchin Denny. I started at eighteen as a messenger boy/clerk and I went through the office for two years, becoming a red button, then a blue button. I loved it.'

The attraction for Jeremy wasn't the dealing with vast sums of money.

'I just liked the whole [philosophy] . . . it was almost military, about your standards, your ethics, how you spoke to people and how you looked: it was all part of the ethos of working in the Stock Exchange.'

In his immaculate suit, silk handkerchief tucked into his breast pocket, it's easy to see why he was drawn in. That initial excitement still hasn't worn off.

'The buzz is being able to see people, talk to people, have our different ideas. I don't want to go and pick up leaves in the garden every day. It gives me a thrill, and I love talking to people – it's not just P+L [profit and loss], it is sharing responsibility and sharing the day together.'

Today's market is a wilder beast, he feels, bemoaning the facelessness of dealing anonymously and the loss of general etiquette.

'My attitude was always much more about enjoying the customer, enjoying the client, enjoying the company. In some ways I'm much too gentle for today's sort of spivvery, but [the City has] stood me in great stead. I still enjoy every penny of it, and my friends do too.'

One of the new guard of faceless traders is Damien

Walsh (not his real name), who cut his teeth at the feet of one of the City's most famous futures dealers.

'I wasn't really sure what I wanted to do after university, but I had a comfort with numbers, and the opportunity presented itself to go into trading. I had a few interviews with a couple of trading houses and I just fell into it. The only reason I went into finance was a suggestion from my parents, who were just exasperated at my indecision career-wise – and I was decent at maths.'

His personality was perfectly suited to the cut and thrust of taking on the market; he never looked back.

'Trading isn't like the rest of finance,' he says. 'You always hear that the traders in a bank are seen as a bit of a different breed and you have to be a lot more independent; it's a lot of pressure, but also you know that, if you succeed, you get to reap all the rewards directly.'

Walsh has no problem with the way traders are remunerated, believing the salary system to truly reflect the inherent worth of each individual doing battle on the screens.

'All work is incentive-based to a certain extent, and all salaries are based on how much you're worth, so if traders get the most amount of money they must be worth something. People are paid what they deserve, and there's no question who gets paid the most amount of money.'

Days one to thirty were a watch-and-learn process, he says, soaking up the atmosphere and trying to decipher the art of staking vast sums at the touch of a button.

'I began by sitting and watching the guy who taught me how to trade, asking him questions until he told me to shut up. In your first month you're looking at someone watching a whole load of prices, who's trading those prices very actively, because we were day traders, putting on very short-term trades from a second to a day. The target was to go home flat at night. So it's a huge amount of information to take in. A first day is a complete washout because you know you're so far from what you're going to need to know in order to be able to put on your first trade.'

Before he could go live, his new-found knowledge was put to work against simulators, in the same way that pilots and astronauts find their feet in the run-up to their maiden voyages.

'They've recorded the markets and they play them back to you, and you fuck about on them to try and get a feel, because, although there's a lot of technical analysis, most traders will say that it's as much about your feel for the market; seeing patterns that aren't necessarily mathematical patterns but appear patterns to the naked eye.'

By the time he was ready to put down money on his first trade he'd been finely tuned by his bosses, until they believed him to be worthy of staking the firm's cash. However, according to Coline Covington, a former chair of the British Psychoanalytic Society, the traits that managers might be looking to exploit in new recruits are not necessarily compatible with what leaders in other employment environments would deem suitable.

'Because [as a screen-based trader] you don't have this one-to-one interaction with people so much, and because you can do it on your own, what's interesting is that it could tend to attract people who tend to be psychopathic. People who have no conscience, who have no concern for other people,' she observes. 'They may be charming, they may be gamblers – most of them are – and omnipotent, but have no real feelings and attachment for other people, no real concern for them. For those types it would be kind of an ideal job.'

Encouraging newcomers to the trading room to put all their emotional eggs in one basket and believe they are waging war on their firm's behalf is an incredibly potent, but dangerous, set of values to instil. Those dealing the companies' cash around the clock are trained to act as attack dogs for their masters; risking their careers and their firms' funds to swell the coffers of the partners and shareholders at all costs.

In such clement conditions for losing touch with the real world, as well as with the traders' own underlying emotional needs and feelings, it is little wonder that the City ends up producing figures responsible for some of the most spectacular falls from grace: whether on a personal level – losing everything they had via a descent into drink or drugs hell – or by dragging down the firms entrusting them with their money, such as the Nick Leesons, Jerome Kerviels and John Rusnaks of this world.

3. The Long and Short of It

Hunched over his glass of perfectly chilled Chablis as we wait for the main courses to arrive, Rob Davis (not his real name) fixes me with a hangdog gaze.

'No one really gets it,' he begins, with the air of a baleful late-night drinker slurring to the barmaid about his wife. 'The general public do not know what hedging is – my friends still don't know what a hedge fund does, and I've tried to tell them for ten years.'

I murmur in sympathy, paying attention as he waxes lyrical about the finer points of what he does for a living.

'A hedge fund's exactly what it says it is: a long/short fund, hedging people's bets,' he continues. 'I'm allowed to be maximum eighty/twenty: eighty long, twenty short. And the other way round. I've still got to always have some kind of hedge on. So if I think the market's going up, I might go sixty-five/thirty-five, because I'm not convinced. But if I'm really sure, say if the market's just had a massive fall, I'll go eighty/twenty.'

I'm happy to listen, although four years earlier my one-track mind would have made it a different story. We're sitting in the low-lit opulence of Locanda Locatelli, a favourite haunt of mine during my trading days, so much so that I could make my way blindfold from the table to the gents: a couple of chicanes past fellow diners, through two doors – one glass, one wooden – and then to the far end of the row of cubicles, where I'd decamp between courses for a dose of my own off-menu palate-cleanser.

The inner workings of a hedge fund meant little to me back then. I only saw hedge-fund traders as a different, mightier species than us low-level brokers, who stalked the same terrain but left footprints far wider and deeper in the scorched earth of the market floor upon which we all dwelt in semi-symbiotic harmony.

Breaking down the City into its component parts and understanding how each piece fits together is a pre-requisite for anyone attempting to decipher the machin-ations of the stock market. But it would take a vast tract of writing to explain all this in substantive terms. Instead I will try to characterize various sectors of City industry and define what sets them apart.

Davis's grievance that no one on the outside under-stands his line of work is a common complaint in the Square Mile. It's hardly surprising, given the superficial-ity with which the general public is encouraged by the press to treat the City. For this book I interviewed prop traders, sales traders, futures traders, fund managers, private client brokers, hedge-fund managers, market makers, inter-dealer brokers and the chief executive of a corporate finance house, among others. Most of these job titles would engender no more than blank stares from anyone outside City circles. But they each play vital, shaping roles in the financial ecosystem, and if the people behind the trading screens are to be understood, their activities must at least be vaguely comprehended.

Davis and his hedge fund is as good a place to start as any. We meet in the classy Italian Locanda Locatelli, in the heart of the West End, rather than in a City restaur-ant, because Park Lane and Mayfair have usurped the Square Mile to become the spiritual home of the hedge-fund community. Hedge funds have been in existence for the best part of sixty years, yet only in recent times have they shot to prominence, thanks to the democratization of the stock market and the massive increase in global trading volumes in equities and derivative products. Hedge funds are much maligned by a sceptical public, who have been led to believe that they are simply gargantuan murky entities lurking in the shadows, emerging from lairs solely to tear chunks out of unsuspecting companies and indices, leaving them battered and bruised or bleeding to death.

The truth, of course, is far less skewed; if it wasn't, hedge funds would have been outlawed long ago by both popular and regulatory demand. Davis, for example, runs a $200 million mini-fund as one member of a team handling several billion dollars of client money, and is ¬ in essence – no different from a pension fund manager. He is freed from some of the shackles that govern long-only funds (which can only take 'long' positions, buying shares in the hope that their price rises), in the sense that he can go short of individual stocks, or the market itself, if he feels a downward move is on the cards.

Many hedge funds (though not Davis's) use gearing to leverage the power of their underlying cash, meaning that they can trade quantities of shares far larger than the funds under their management. Leverage allows greater potential returns to the investor than otherwise would have been available, but the potential for loss is also greater because, if the investment becomes worthless, the loan principal and all accrued interest on the loan still need to be repaid. Despite the increased flexibility that gearing provides, ultimately hedge funds are restricted by their own set of rules just as strict as those of other market players.

'Every trade's got parameters, so my parameters are that I run $200 million, and I'm allowed maximum position size of 7, 10 per cent of my whole fund [i.e. no individual trade can exceed a tenth of the overall funds under his control],' Davis explains. 'The fund's not leveraged, so for every pound I put down, there's a pound in cash. You can't break parameters. If I went and bought $20.01 million of a stock an alarm would ring. [Risk managers are] like working with a policeman behind you all the time.'

Since Davis is responsible for enormous sums of money, in comparison to the kind of sums being staked by private individuals and their brokers on the same markets, it is no surprise that his activity is so strictly monitored. At the same time he is backed by a seriously professional arsenal of human and computerized research, which gives him the confidence to lay seven- and eight-figure trades.

'SEEK [his fund's exclusive system] is like a research tool – I can show you on my phone. I've got Bloomberg on my phone, and to complement it we have SEEK. SEEK sets off alerts, and it generates trading pattern ideas. We have another system called TAKE, which feeds off SEEK: we've got some quants guys who do that kind of thing. They literally get signals: "buy this immediately", "this stock's broken out, buy it now".'

The sophistication of the programmes which hedge funds – and other mammoth funds of investor cash – use to make trading decisions is light years away from how the markets originally operated, and the decoupling of the interests of investors and the companies in which they invest has caused no end of bitterness. In 1990 Sir Hector Laing, the departing chairman of United Biscuits,

was already taking aim at those in the City making a living trading companies' shares: 'Fund managers are intent
on doing their best for their funds and have no interest
whatsoever in the business they invest in or the people
who are producing the profits,' he complained. 'The stock
market is coming to be less a means of allocating capital
to productive use, than and end unto itself – a computer
game for those who compete in the "finance league".
But it is an eroding game, which undermines the true
value of the counters with which it is being played – the
national industrial and commercial base.'

Laing's line of thinking is shared by countless market
Luddites, who bemoan the way in which the stock market's inherent purpose has been so radically altered. What
once was simply a way for companies to raise capital
from the investing public has, they say, morphed into the
largest casino on earth, with speculators and gamblers
punting on anything from pork belly futures to carbon
emission permits without concern about the underlying
commodity they are trading.

However, fund managers and traders are not simply
one homogeneous mass, effecting glorified bets. There is
a reason that they and banking houses handle vast
amounts of public and private wealth: there is a method
to the madness.

Short-term trading as opposed to long-term investing
may leave a bad taste in the mouths of its detractors, but
– as with hedge funds, leveraging and all of the other
myriad 'new breed' of market strategy – it is entirely
legitimate under market rules, and thus not worthy of the
demonic tag that it has acquired. If there was something
fundamentally illicit about the practice, it would have
been strangled at birth by the authorities, but instead it is

recognized as just as permissible an activity as any of the plethora of investment models. Prop traders – the shorthand for those doing proprietary trading with funds belonging to their firm itself, rather than the firm's clients – are more often than not remunerated according to their performance at the end of the year, a system which accounts for the tales of six-, seven- and eight-figure bonuses pounced upon by an eager press every winter.

Rob Davis operates under a similar system at his hedge fund and believes the pay structure to be far purer, and more honest, than that of private client brokers, for example. Having worked in the broking industry himself during his early City career, he is well placed to understand the fundamental flaws in brokerage fees.

'I have an issue with my old job,' he explains, 'because, in difficult markets like we have at present, if I put a hundred grand with a broker, and now the stock market's down 40 per cent, if my broker's performed in line with the market, then my hundred grand's now sixty grand – but the broker's still trading. And I think to myself, he's got clients losing money, but he's still earning commission.

'Some brokers will actually earn more money than me this year, but aren't making money for their clients. I think that's an absolute con. There are brokers out there who will say, "It's the 29th of October, I haven't done much commission this month, so I'll switch my clients out of Invensys into Vodafone and make five grand commission." That's criminal – we've seen it in full flow. The fact that [a broker friend] is saying he had his best-ever month when his clients are losing fortunes means there's something wrong. I think the whole City should be performance-related.'

Davis only earns serious money when he's making positive returns for the fund's investors, incentivizing him to be careful with every trade.

'I'm getting paid on what I make, and that's how it should be. We don't get paid a wage in the hedge-fund business; in a hedge fund it's called being "below your watermark". Say you start at zero and make two million, you're up two million [and get paid a percentage of the profit as reward]. Say you then lose three million, you're now down a million overall, which you then have to make back, along with another two million, in order to be above your high watermark. You have to make back three million [in total, before you earn another penny for yourself]. That's why for fund managers it can be a very scary time, because you can be down, and you can get more down and more down and more down, and you think there's no way back.'

Steven Gold, the private client investment manager, maintains that losing money does affect him, although the damage is more to his pride than his pocket.

'You can go home one day and you've had a really good day, been busy; you've bought something that's done really well and you've taken a profit. But you can also go home the next day and feel terribly depressed because you've lost your clients' money.'

Gold's take on the market leans more towards the old guard.

'The main purpose of the stock market has always been to raise capital, so new companies coming on to the market raise capital to expand, and entrepreneurs cash in and give someone a chance to buy into their business. But the secondary market is clearly a function of having investments or assets – an asset class. You've got bonds, you've got property, you've got cash, you've got stocks, and that gives you a chance to invest part of your pension, part of your personal money, into the well-being of companies.'

He believes that investors buying stock in a company actually aid the firm in expanding their share of the market place, marking out shareholders as almost philanthropic and benevolent in their actions.

'You have to remember the higher a company's share price, the more chance that company's got of getting more business, growing. A successful company with a strong share price can go to other companies that they're trying to do business with and get that deal done. Whereas with weak companies with very weak share prices, someone might not want to trade with them because they might think they're a bad credit risk.'

Ultimately, however, he is under no illusion about his own purpose in the wider scheme. 'Most of what I do is actually creating a chance for people to get returns on their money that are different to, say, putting it into bonds or cash. Crudely speaking, I'm trying to make people wealthier. That's the bottom line of what I do.'

In that sense, he is no different from Davis, or anyone else employed to turn water into wine on their clients' behalf. Whether advising clients on safe havens for their pensions during turbulent markets or opening three-minute-long trading positions on a prop book, the underlying intention is always the same.

Yet, when the two worlds collide, the friction between those in opposing camps leaves bad blood. When I worked with Jeremy Lyon, who was schooled in the nobler art of people-led broking rather than screen-based dealing, a culture clash temporarily severed our working ties. He

had a long-established position as a middleman between
the wholesale and retail sides of the business, straddling
the divide between the market makers (who set prices in
stocks and sell them in bulk to brokers) and the brokers
themselves, who filled orders on behalf of their clients
outside the City sphere.

Whilst much of my trading business was screen-based
– requiring me to simply place an order on the SETS
order book at the touch of a button – dealing in smaller,
non-SETS companies required a more delicate approach,
which was where Lyon came in. It felt as though he
knew each and every market maker out there, which
wasn't far from the truth, since market making is very
much a closed circuit, built upon foundations of close-
contact and face-to-face relationships struck up while
socializing. I could pick up the STX phones and deal in
a straightforward fashion – reading the price off the
screen and just getting an order completed at the going
market price. But Lyon's expertise was knowing who
might have cheaper stock on offer, who would be able to
fill an outsized order and who was making a price out of
duty but would prefer not to deal, perhaps because they
were having a bad run on their own book, and selling
more stock would only exacerbate their misfortune.

One afternoon, Lyon having been part of a deal to
place an overhang of stock in a small technology company amongst clients willing to mop up the shares at
eighteen pence each, I waded into the fray on behalf of
a client who wanted to trade the same stock. The price
was now nineteen pence to sell, nineteen and a quarter
to buy, but the day's heavy volume was alerting other
traders as well, and the price was threatening to continue
moving upwards before I'd dealt.

Lyon found me a few hundred thousand shares from a client willing to reduce his position and bank a 7 per cent return for a few minutes' work, but by the time we came to agreement on the trade, the mid-price had already jumped to twenty pence and rising. Jeremy told me that the price we would deal at would be twenty, rather than nineteen and an eighth, which infuriated my client no end, since he was only looking for a 5 or 6 per cent return from the trade and would be a seller himself at twenty pence.

I took up the charge on behalf of my client, entering into a screaming match with Lyon that only ended when we were hauled into the dealing-room manager's office. Lyon had acted far more magnanimously than me, as was his way, yet had stood his ground, before losing patience and telling me I could have it my way – 'But you'd better not ever come to me to do your business again.' Even at the height of my rage, I knew better than to enter into that pact, recognizing that, without the deftness of his dealing, my ability to service my clients' needs would be mortally undermined. Whilst in the short term my only care was getting my client's order done so that he could take a few thousand pounds' profit from a five-minute trade, there was no way I could sacrifice my working relationship with my elder and better, since even the client concerned would lose out in the long run.

Looking back, that flare-up epitomized the dichotomy between the old- and new-school approaches to the market. Whilst very low-key and parochial in the wider scheme of things, the chasm that temporarily opened up between Lyon and me embodied more than just a difference in thinking between two types of broker or two types of client. Five years on, and still plying his trade as adroitly as ever before, Lyon makes no bones about the danger of anonymous traders doing battle over screens, whose ethics are sidelined in place of a 'get rich or die trying' stampede towards instant returns.

We meet for lunch in Moorgate, joined by Roy Cutts, another veteran of the market's pre-Big Bang days, who has known and loved Lyon for decades, and the feeling is most assuredly mutual. As we stroll down the busy mid-day streets in the weak, wintry sunshine, Lyon and Cutts are greeted like celebrities by passing City folk. We duck into City Boot, a wood-panelled watering hole. 'The clientele,' according to Cutts, 'are brokers, fund managers, bon viveurs, raconteurs and general wags.' The pair are well received in here as well, stopping to exchange greetings with pinstripe-sporting peers at tables heaving under the weight of pint and wine glasses.

Once the Chardonnay is flowing at our own table, they hark back to the good old days of the Stock Exchange floor, swapping old war stories.

'Remember when we were fighting Greenwell?' Cutts recalls, with a twinkle in his eye. 'I got my eyes ripped out by Morgan around that time . . .' he continues, conjuring up images of a bygone era when it was all about who you knew and how you dealt, rather than how sharp your hand–eye coordination was. Dealing on the floor was 'such a joy', according to Lyon; 'simply wonderful', in Cutts's words.

The lack of ethics in today's climate is a contentious issue, with both men spitting blood as they highlight the insouciance and ingratitude of many of the latest generation of dealers.

'The market's changed for the worse,' comments Cutts. 'The Stock Exchange motto was "my word is my bond", and it doesn't exist any more amongst a lot of the youngsters, unfortunately. It's not like a club as it was; if you were naughty on the floor you would soon get found out. I know people that have been barred from the floor over their dealing etiquette. Once you lost your reputation, it would take a long time to get it back, but dealing over the telephone now and on the machines, it's much easier to be a little naughtier, because you're more anonymous.'

One aspect of the democratization of the City in the eighties was opening up the markets to people who previously would not have found it accessible. With the loss of the invisible red velvet rope came the feeling that it was every man for himself, and a loosening of the ties that previously bound brokers to jobbers and kept good manners high on the list of dealing-floor requirements.

Whilst delighting in bawdy, unrestrained gossiping and ribaldry in private, away from the STX lines, Lyons and Cutts are both careful when it comes to how they do business. Prefacing phone conversations with 'quote only' or 'price and size please' can be the difference between simply getting a feel for the market in a certain stock and being unceremoniously 'stuffed' by a dealer with stock to sell if the wrong phraseology is employed. They both feel that there is little that can be done to school today's traders in the mannerisms and standards of yesteryear.

'You can't really say this is how we used to do it because it wouldn't mean a thing to them,' says Cutts. 'What you could say is look, this is how it works and this is how it should be done.'

They began life as blue buttons, 'which was described as the lowest form of animal life on the floor of the Stock Exchange,' laughs Cutts. 'You were a runner, going round checking prices. Nothing was electronic; you just put the prices down on your paper, went round to get the whole lot, got back to the office and the prices were typed on a skin, on a Roneo machine [precursor to photocopiers]. The names of the stock were typed on the skin, and I'd fill in the bid and offer prices, then put it on the machine, roll off twenty copies and then I'd take them round to some of the institutions. There were some outside phones on the floor, but normally it would be done via the office, and the office would then get on to the Stock Exchange, and the waiter would call you. The waiters used to be on stands in the market; they'd have different areas of the market, and they'd blow through pipes like they had on boats in the old days. The whistle would go, the waiter would put it to his ear and listen, and if it was for me he'd call out, "Roy Cutts, five double seven." Then the light would go up, and you knew you were wanted on the phone.'

Such a process is unimaginable to today's traders, who demand instant access to prices, graphs and account balances, not to mention dedicated lines to dealers. Now time is money, and timing is everything. The opening up of the market to investors on every continent means that there is no space for social niceties when filling orders; as Lyons puts it: 'It's so wide now that you're getting people in Japan gambling in things here when they should be fast asleep. The City has totally changed; it's now a world market rather than just a London market or a New York market. Such is the communication – you just can't imagine how international funds now are in unison. You keep on reading about Wall Street being up 2.5 per cent, Germany up 2 per cent ... London still dominates some markets, insurance and shipping are the two major ones, where, if you don't deal in London or don't check the price in London, you're going to get a poorer deal. But world equity markets and bond markets are now in operation virtually twenty-four hours a day. The result is that confidence builds up too much, and people think the screen is telling them everything. Well it's not.'

Stock Exchange announcements – company results, trading updates, shareholding shifts, interest rates – are simultaneously broadcast on thousands of screens in scores of countries; in Lyon's and Cutts's day the process was far more tortuous.

'There'd be a notice, and you'd get the figures back to your office as quickly as possible,' says Cutts. 'There was some form of ticker tape, and you would get news out on that, it would come off and they'd pin it up on one of the boards in the Stock Exchange.'

Consequently, results and announcements were not the main mover of prices then; instead it was down to simple 'buying and selling, or the jobbers moving prices [to try to stimulate interest and activity in the stock]', he explains.

'A wise man once said to me, "Roy, if you check your price around the market and everybody's making five and threepence to five and sixpence, you can guarantee one thing – they are not five and threepence to five and sixpence, and it's up to you as the broker to find out what the real price is." Which you did by prodding, asking for a price and size, and so on.'

Having friends and trusted confidants in the market was key to a broker's or dealer's success, requiring a keen sense of camaraderie and a willingness to strike up relationships with peers across the board.

'As a blue button it's a little more difficult,' says Cutts, 'but as a dealer that's when you make your contacts, and you couldn't be a dealer in those days until you were twenty-one. You used to go out a little bit [with fellow dealers] in the evening; you would have a drink and a chat with them at lunchtimes in all the bars around the Stock Exchange. You had to be fairly outgoing – you couldn't be a wallflower, otherwise people wouldn't get to know you, would they?'

Since the switch from floor trading to electronic dealing, the significance of people-based knowledge gathering has diminished, with traders relying on other methods to gauge the feel of a certain stock or index. As soon as a trade is completed, it is printed on the screen (with some exceptions), allowing traders to see how much volume is taking place and at what price the deals are being done.

'The screen is so revealing, and you have to mark your bargain so quickly,' notes Lyons, 'whereas we didn't mark our bargains until the end of the day, so no one knew what we'd done. Nowadays, just because someone's done a couple of million Vodafone at this price, someone like Rothschilds or another of the big boys says, "Oh, well, he's done two million, so I want to do two million as well" – you could never do that back then. The restraint on you was such that you were far better controlled and you didn't take those sorts of risks.'

Relying on intraday graphs to predict future share price movements was unheard of as well; the only way to work out which way the stock would move next was by weighing up the style and form of the individuals doing the buying and selling.

'You knew who the buyers and the sellers were; the brokers, at least – you didn't actually know the end client. So if someone you knew was sharp comes and says,

"Jeremy, I want the offer of some Granada," you'd know by the number of times he's dealt with you that one, he'll want to deal, and two, he's pretty likely to be hot, so don't mess with him. Whereas if you get some strange little old woman coming out from Belfast saying, "I want the price and size of 25,000 Granadas for six quid," it would be amateurish, and you'd know that you're not gonna get picked up. With the sharp broker, you'd just be careful or you'd follow them: you'd say, well, I'll sell you twenty-five and keep twenty-five, and, blow me down, they'll want to get the price better, won't they? And you were ready.'

The longer our lunch went on, the more it dawned on me how wide the gulf was between the market today and the long-lost era to which they harked back. The most acute difference was in the type of memories they shared between themselves: whilst they discussed people and places, my friends and I discussed our greatest trades in terms of how fast-fingered we had been, measuring our prowess by the same yardstick we'd used when crowing about our Nintendo skills during our school days.

Sitting in Damien Walsh's Primrose Hill flat, all the trappings of his success surrounding him – expansive leather sofas, outsized plasma television, lit-up tropical fishtank glowing warmly from the corner of the room – just such computer-game rivalry comes to the fore. After I regale him with tales of my top-scoring trades, he sits forward and visibly brightens as he recalls his crowning moment in the futures market.

'The trade I was most proud of came during a non-farm payrolls [announcement], which used to be the biggest economic figure – things now have moved on substantially in the last three years, and it's not very relevant any more. But five, six years ago, that first Friday of every month was the most intense two minutes of anything that happened. Maybe – if it was the big one – it was the biggest thing of the year, unless a war broke out or there was a terrorist attack or something.

'I was market-making in Eurodollars and I was trading a huge amount. I basically traded about 50,000 lots on about twenty-five, thirty different products on three computers across twenty-four screens, all in the space of about three and a half minutes. I must have clicked the mouse 100, 150 times in those two or three minutes and on every one of them I could have lost tens of thousands of pounds, but I got it all right – and it was so important that I got it all right: getting any one of them wrong would have ruined the whole thing, and I didn't. And that's how right it has to go sometimes.'

Just hearing him excitedly tell the story gets my juices flowing, recalling the thrill of being actively involved in a wildly gyrating stock or index, an experience as hair-raising as trying to hurl a race car round a blind corner. I countered with another of my personal favourite trades, when I hit all the stock on the bid side of the SETS orderbook a split second after the company concerned had issued a profits warning, an action that, while legal, was dubious in terms of etiquette, since it would have been more proper to allow the bid order to be pulled in the wake of the announcement.

In Damien's view, however, the screens are a dog-eat-dog environment, and there is scant room for sentiment.

'In futures there isn't a "you should let the bid get pulled" mindset, because the bid getting pulled is the same shit. It's all just trading.'

We discuss whether our achievements on the trading

platforms would impress those outside the world of the markets, aware that only a select few could understand the underlying technique involved.

'I can see that there's something to be proud of in the trade you did, because I'm a trader,' he says. 'Though I can see how other people don't understand what's so great about that. But they can't possibly deny the kind of information flow that you have to deal with when you're making a decision like that. That's what I consider; that's something to be proud of, you know? Getting something absolutely fucking right. And for me it has to be something a bit more than just making a bit of money. For me that something was getting the job done at all. A job that probably should have theoretically taken ten, twenty people, and I did it by myself.'

Jonny White (not his real name), a no-nonsense sales trader at a Canary Wharf-based American bank, bridges the gap between trader and broker in his work, having to both garner business and execute the resulting orders in the same hyper-fast-moving world of index futures that Damien inhabits.

'I'm a salesman in effect, if you want to put it like that, selling futures,' he begins.

His description of futures is far from easy to follow, reflecting the casualness with which a twenty-year veteran approaches the underlying product he's sold round the clock every day of his career.

'A future is a derivative product. Take a Big Mac – wherever you go round the world, that Big Mac never changes, but the prices may be different, also the price can fluctuate on supply and demand. If nobody round the world wants Big Macs, the Big Mac price will come off; if everybody in the world wants a Big Mac, the price

will go up; and that's exactly macro supply and demand.
All of a sudden, there's a problem with the price of pickled cucumbers. Well, they have to have pickled cucumbers in a Big Mac, so all of a sudden there's a derivative of
that Big Mac. If there's trouble with cucumbers, the price
of futures will go up. Because when you come to delivery
of futures, you're getting a Big Mac with everything in it,
regardless of the problems with the pickled cucumbers.
You're buying a Big Mac and that's what futures are, ultimately – standardized products which float up and down
in price depending on various factors.'

In simpler terms, a futures contract gives the holder
the obligation to make or take delivery of the underlying
asset at a certain date, depending on whether they are the
buyer or seller. Historically, futures were used to help
farmers fix a price for their produce, so that they could
properly budget for their year's expenses without having
to worry about fluctuating prices. Wheat futures could be
sold by the farmer at two dollars per bushel, guaranteeing
that – come harvest time – he knew he would be able to
offload the wheat at a fixed price to an agreed buyer.

The first recorded futures contracts were made in
Japan in the eighteenth century, to meet the needs of
Samurai who, having been paid in rice, and after a series
of bad harvests, needed a stable conversion to coin. Now,
of course, futures trading is not the exclusive preserve of
food producers, mineral extractors or oil companies;
futures are bought and sold by institutional and private
traders with no interest in actual delivery of the underlying commodity. The vast majority of futures never
reach delivery date, instead being simply matched off
against contrary futures contracts, with the profit or loss
being taken by those either side of the bargain.

'Our clients use futures for either hedging purposes or speculative purposes,' says White. 'One thing about futures is that there's no bar or ban on short-selling. There are futures that are on equity indices, like the FTSE index, so if you think the FTSE's going down but you're banned from short-selling shares, you go and sell the futures instead. Futures on financials and equities are traded on [four] quarterlies: December, March, June and September. So right now we're trading for December, and then when December expires we're trading for March.'

He is as at home in the world of screen-based futures as Lyon and Cutts are in their face-to-face community of equity dealing, warming to his theme as he describes his everyday business.

'Daily activity is to bring clients in who trade futures, and every lot of futures they trade I make commission, so I'm getting clients into that trade as much as possible to bring commission into our P+L. Number one, it's not ultimately what you know, it's who you know over many years. So, for example, I've got a friend who's a convertible bond trader and uses futures to sometimes speculate, but mostly hedge [his book]. If he knows he's long a lot of equities, he thinks, "What do I do to hedge it, to make sure it all comes off? I sell futures to the market," so if the market moves against him, he's kind of safe with his money.'

White's expertise, rather like mine was as an advisory broker, is in the way he handles his clients' accounts and takes care of their every need.

'They can go to whoever they want, to whoever gives the best value. I don't just say, "Use me, and I'll simply buy one, sell one," I write information, I write commentary on the markets, what I think, how I feel. I send out research coming from our bank's analysts, who're some of the best in the City – and also some of the worst. I don't like analysts personally, they're all wankers . . . So I'm sending out flow, sending out what I think other people are doing, and because of that colour, because I'm giving him information, they think, "I wanna give Jonny a bit of business."

'Also there is a bit of cronyism. A guy I've known for twenty years in the City, he'll look after his mate. I'm the same – if I'm going to give business out in metals futures, I give it to a friend. I do have to look after other people, but I give it to a friend of mine because it's about looking after the people who look after you, the people who send you the right information.'

To White, the hardest part of the business is getting clients in the first place; after that, it's all plain sailing.

'If I call the markets, it's my opinion. That bit's easy. I've always got an opinion, and it doesn't matter if you're wrong; if you've got an opinion it's good, because you have to remember that the client will make his own decision, whatever you say. He wants to hear what you think, what's going on, who's speaking, what you think of interest rates, what's Paulson said yesterday about the TARP . . . There're things going on all the time. In futures you're on specialized desks – financial futures, options; some just do execution, but my desk is multi-products.

'I'm doing equities, I'm doing commodities. Whoever I pick up a line to, I've got to know what I'm talking about instantly,' he says, snapping his fingers together. 'That's the stress of being aware of what's going on around you, and the art of bullshit. If you don't know, bullshit it – and if you really don't know, say you don't know. A lot of the time you can bullshit – that's what people do.'

Once the clients have given White an order, the job is far from over.

'Futures are exchange-traded, it's on a screen. It used to be on the LIFFE [London International Financial Futures and Options Exchange] floor, when if you wanted to trade you rang down to the floor. There'd be a guy on the phone, he'd signal to a guy in the pit, who would find a trader in the middle of that pit, signal back to you, and that was it. That's all gone. Now it's on the screens, at the click of a mouse. I execute my own orders.

'At our bank there are three main trading floors. The first floor is just pure equities and equity derivatives; the second floor is fixed income, which is all of the financial products – interest rates, foreign exchange, bonds, swaps, government stuff; and there's the third floor, which is commodities, futures and the finance desk. So we are on the quieter floor compared to the others. Me and the guy I work with, we've got about eighteen screens and keyboards everywhere, because it's all for different systems. That's the excitement. A lot of testosterone goes on, because you're in a greed environment.'

The images White conjures up of his trading floor bring to mind Lord Healey's 1993 description of the interior landscape of the City: '[We talk about the markets] as though they were God in heaven, but they are numerous men in red braces in dealing rooms who talk cockney, working for a lot of men in grey suits with red bow ties.' Whilst the stereotypes of Healey's portrait have been updated during the intervening fifteen years, their underlying purpose has not changed – short-term speculating in a high-pressure, high-octane environment.

To be fair to today's traders, they are only continuing a decades-old City tradition; for all that Lyon's and

Cutts's early years were spent in a far less manic, far more people-based climate, they were as much enslaved to the conventions of short-term trading as those who came after them. That side of the market comes with the territory; John Ruskin was already taking aim at speculators over a century ago: 'While real commerce is founded on real necessities or uses, and limited by these, speculation, of which the object is merely gain, seeks to excite imaginary necessities and popular desires in order to gather its temporary profit from the supply of them.'

4. 'One for the Boys'

The City's public image is tarnished even at the best of times, thanks to perennial cultural references to illegal activity and endemic insider dealing in the Square Mile. A string of infamous 'rogue traders' have shown that this perception is based on far more than simple urban myths. But this remains an off-limits conversation topic for most in the City, except among tight-knit groups of colleagues after hours.

Even with my insider access to traders at all levels, only one person I spoke to was prepared to admit to regular personal involvement in illicit trading: Dexter Williams (not his real name), a well-spoken stockbroker in his mid-thirties. However, his testimony does show how easy it has been for traders to circumvent the authorities and abuse the system. And Williams speaks with a defiant air, his attitude being 'everyone else was doing it, so why shouldn't I?'

Williams describes how traders can use dummy accounts and illegally hive off profits from deals. In essence this was a hybrid of Nick Leeson's 88888 account (the one Leeson utilized to hide his losses from his employers) and that of an everyday private client, which Williams used to line his own pockets whenever the opportunity arose.

He begins with a story which 'was no different from what we could pull off on any of the other 364 days in the year', he claims. 'My partner on the adjoining desk to mine was convinced a bid was coming for Company A. But he was like the boy who cried wolf – every five minutes he'd get a text, or a call, or even just a vision, about this or that company being the subject of a take-over bid. Nine times out of ten it was complete balls – but, in this game, balls wins prizes. Because, if you buy early, and the story reaches enough people, the stock's going to fly – truth or no truth – and you've sold yours well before the company issues a denial announcement.'

Hard facts mean little in a world ruled by paranoia and fear, as I know all too well from my trading days – paranoia that everyone's trying to do you out of your profit, and fear that you're going to miss out on even bigger winnings if you don't follow the herd. People like Dexter's partner acted as both instigators and reactors in this game: some days they'd get the ball rolling when they felt like ramping a stock; on other days they'd be just one more adding to the Chinese whispers that blew round the City like wind through rushes.

'So, for all that I doubted his latest rumour, I agreed to keep my eye on the screens, in case anything did happen. We worked well like that – he had all the sources, I did the grunt work. That's the way it went. Bang – Company A announces it's received an approach. My fingers knew what they were doing before my eyes had caught up. Buy ... 100,000 ... limit, say, £9.55. Got them – now we're off and running,' he continues, visibly thrilled to be back in the moment as he retells his larceny-laced tale. 'Ten seconds later and the little beauties were changing hands at £10.25, no ... £10.35, £10.40 ... £10.50 now ... I was yelping like a puppy, and sold back the 100,000 I'd just bought for £10.52. We erupted like Vesuvius, which was fair enough, given that we were sitting on nearly a hundred grand profit between the two of us.'

So far, so legal. However: 'The rules say you must specify which client you're dealing for before you trade – so, in theory, the Company A winnings would already have had a home. But, for many a broker, the rules are slightly different. You trade first, ask questions later. If it all goes wrong, if the stock falls instead of rises, there's always a pension fund or discretionary account that can take the hit for £50,000 or so. But if – with Company A, for example – you hit the jackpot, then fuck the clients, this one's for the boys.

'Everyone had dummy punters, friends or relatives who let you wash winners through their account. So in the case of Company A and a two-man team, this would mean just shy of a hundred grand split two ways: more than £45,000 apiece – less 40 per cent capital gains tax, and that would be nearly thirty grand each,' he explains, staring defiantly at me as the details sink in.

'I had a setup with a friend who didn't work in the City. We'd go sixty-forty on each deal – but I had to see it in cash the same day, and of course I took the sixty. His account was entirely governed by me. I had tacit approval to move as much stock through it as I liked, so long as he was always up at the end of the week. And that's what I did. The compliance department [company employees who were answerable to the FSA, who were supposed to check that all the deals were above board] barely batted an eyelid at his account's stellar performance, assuming he was a proper punter who knew the ropes – plus I threw in a few losing trades every now and then to throw them off the scent.

'I could take six-figure positions in his name with

ease. Whatever smash and grab I pulled off would soon
be marked down on a dealing ticket with his name and
number at the top; I passed the ticket to the boys in the
back office, who put the trade into the system, thus
ensuring the cash made its way to its (not so) rightful
home. A few hours after banking our profit on Company A, I was picking up my haul in folding bills some-
where near Marylebone High Street.'

Warming to his theme, Williams asks why he shouldn't
dip his fingers in the cookie jar like everyone else.

'In my first week in the job, it was beautifully summed
up for me,' he recalls. 'One of the brokers on our desk told
me, "If you've got a son who's a doctor, then he'll give you
a free check-up when you need one. If your dad's a lawyer,
he'll do your conveyancing for nothing, won't he? So if
your best friend's a broker, you'd expect him to toss you
free money when it's on offer. That's what we do." There's
no point pretending – no one is in this game to make the
world a better place. It's all about the money. From the
bottom up, the only thing that matters is feathering your
own nest, regardless of who gets shafted along the way or
how compromised your morals become in the process.'

Williams has seen first-hand what lies beneath the
façade of London's financial district, as well as having
taken part in the underhand dealings himself with gusto.

'For all that the Stock Exchange is presented as a trans-
parent, trustworthy great British institution, the truth is
that everywhere corruption drips like honey. Despite all
the talk of FSA controls, those working there know they
can get away with abuses with barely a slap on the wrist
– and so they do, day after day, year after year.'

He was perfectly placed to participate in the dot-com
boom at the end of the 1990s.

'Back then, not a day went by without yet another stock doubling in price as the punters piled in,' says Williams, at ease with the picture he has been painting of the dark side of the Square Mile. 'According to one of the bosses one summer, the next big thing was going to be Company B. This was a cash shell – a listed company with some funds on its balance sheet, but otherwise no operational business – and our firm's finance department was negotiating a deal to reverse a new internet company into it, which meant the sky was the limit in terms of its future share price. Officially, there were Chinese walls between the finance department and the trading room, which meant the brokers shouldn't have been privy to any of the impending deals being thrashed out upstairs. In practice there was no such thing – and no one batted an eyelid in the compliance department.'

In such clement conditions for financial chicanery, it seemed to Williams almost par for the course to get involved himself.

'None of the brokers would be so brazen as to trade any "house" stocks in their own account, as their personal trades were far more likely than their clients' to be scrutinized, so most people just bought Company B for their favourite clients and took their cut through the commission they charged.

'Other brokers displayed even more chutzpah, setting up accounts in the names of trusted friends, then washing trades through their accounts and taking their cut of the profits in cash. I told a friend what was going on with the stock – which had risen by now from 50p to more than £2. He loaded up, strapped himself in for the ride, and within a couple of weeks was selling them back to the market at more than £4 apiece. He paid me back handsomely via a few well-stuffed brown envelopes, and we all did very nicely out of the experience.'

Some of Williams's closest friends at other firms were just as deeply involved in the insider dealing 'pandemic', as he calls it.

'It went on round the clock at one firm with a small and exclusive customer base: property tycoons, pop stars and assorted other celebrities. Many sat on the boards of public companies and were more than happy to brief their brokers about their own shares. No matter to them that they were under obligation not to divulge financial information when their firms were in "closed periods"; they used coded signals and texts to get the message out that the time was right to buy or sell their stock, before the public got hold of the information.

'The brokers greedily devoured the morsels they were thrown – after all, being in the know is everything in stock market circles. If a takeover bid was coming for a certain company, you could guarantee those close to the board would have a quiet fifty-grand punt on the stock in the run-up to the event. And when the right people bought, it sent a signal to the partners to fill their own personal accounts with the shares too, before they passed on the tip to their friends in the market and really got the ball rolling.

'The brokers could also rely on their friends at other trading houses to pass on any nuggets that came their way. The brokerage wasn't considered competition by the market colossuses – if anything, they were akin to the birds that feed themselves cleaning hippos' teeth, and the relationship suited both parties. Many of the top traders and market makers at the major firms had their personal accounts with them.

'Technically they were obliged to report their dealings to their own compliance officers, but if another broker-age carried out the trades, there was much less scrutiny of whether they'd put their own interests before those of their clients. They'd call my friend and tell him what to buy in their names, then say, "You should have some of those yourselves; we're about to run the price up." Once everyone was on board, that's exactly what happened. The market is run on a "for us, by us" mentality.'

It wasn't just brokers and their immediate clients who took part in the cloak-and-dagger activities, he maintains.

'There were financial journalists who were just as deeply in the pockets of the industry and broking fig-ures. If the morning papers carried reports of bid rumours for a stock, you knew that whoever was the source of the whisper had already loaded up on stock for themselves.

'For the journalists it was a self-fulfilling prophecy – once they'd reported the story, their readers would wit-ness the meteoric rise of the shares during the course of the day. Any trader who tipped off the City pages' gossip columnists could count on maximum exposure, thus giving their stocks a welcome fillip when the market opened next day. If the story had legs, the company involved would put out a "response to press speculation" announcement and confirm that they were indeed in bid talks – so the shares would rocket, and those already in would be laughing. If the story was false, chances were the price would spike initially as the so-called "mug punters" piled in, giving those who'd bought the day before the chance to offload their stock. And by the time the company denied any bid, the only people left hold-ing the baby were those sucked in by the paper's eager reporting of the rumours.

'Either way, journalists played as important a part as anyone in the ramping of share prices, which is why they were treated with such deference by brokers and company executives alike. 'Buy on rumour, sell on fact' was an adage to which we all stuck – the real moves in price came long before companies issued official guidance about their activities.

'Calls that came through to the dealing room were taped, but mobile phone calls were not; nor were text messages monitored. Chats in local bars and pubs provided equally secure ways to circumvent compliance procedures. These were people who wouldn't steal from the supermarket but thought nothing of the way they robbed the rich to make themselves even richer.

'Every illegally gotten piece of information was depriving outsiders of the chance to trade the markets on a level playing field. For every penny made illicitly, by definition someone had to lose in return. Spoofing the public into buying shares via newspapers or by spreading rumours was highly questionable, but in a world in which morals are defined by the standards of those around you, who would point the finger?' he asks defensively.

The 'City Slickers' affair at the *Daily Mirror* was a high-profile example of the illicit practices of some within the financial media. Anil Bhoyrul and James Hipwell, the paper's City Slickers columnists, were found guilty of market manipulation after using the *Mirror*'s City pages to tip shares in companies in which they owned stock. Editor Piers Morgan was caught up in the scandal too, after he bought 20,000 shares in technology company Viglen a day before City Slickers told readers to buy the stock, causing the shares to double in price. After a DTI investigation, he was cleared of any wrongdoing, but the Slickers themselves did not escape the wrath of the prosecutors.

Slickers aside, the ecosystem worked nicely for all those on the inside of the Square Mile-sized gentlemen's club that Williams inhabited. It wasn't what the FSA had in mind when it periodically promised to clean up the world of finance, but by only monitoring the situation from afar, says Williams, it was never likely to penetrate the opaque sheen that allowed duplicity and double standards to flourish unchecked within broking houses.

'Occasional censures were handed out, but no one I knew was ever caught for their crimes. With neither peer pressure to play fair nor intervention from on high, it's no wonder the City continues to adhere only to the law of the jungle.'

When I question others about how insider dealing is perceived inside the City, the blasé and unconcerned response indicates an absolving of the City of any kind of collective responsibility for the actions of the bad apples in their midst. The feeling appears to be that, yes, it goes on, but there is very little that can be done about it, and, anyway, it doesn't fall on us to keep our peers in line.

Some take it one step further, asserting that, since corruption and imperfection are inherent to the human condition, there is little point getting too hung up on the City's reflection of a wider malaise.

'You know it always goes on, of course,' Michael Parnes says flatly. 'As long as there are humans – and by design we all have our faults – they'll take advantage of situations when they shouldn't. I don't think it's particular to our business, but it will always happen. It will happen in any industry; it just so happens that you perhaps hear about it more at the moment in ours, and it's more serious in the financial business.'

Darren Carver is of a similar view: 'I just think where you've got lawyers and bankers it's going to be there, and of course the onus is on the authorities to prove it. I think it'll always be there. While there's always a way to make a fast buck, there are going to be people that exploit it.'

The regulators, who ought to be stamping out money laundering, insider dealing and market abuse like forest fires wherever they occur, are notoriously slack at taking action. For all its bluster, the FSA – set up to regulate the industry – has a particularly hands-off approach when it comes to addressing the suspicious moves in hundreds of share prices every week. Whilst insider trading – dealing stocks with the benefit of knowledge not available to the public – is strictly illegal, I was told that it is also so rife among City firms as to have become all but institutionalized.

Knowledge is power, and since, in the world of finance, power is money, it's little wonder that, however hard the FSA tries to stamp out the abuse, those who call the shots in the City try even harder to get away with it. In the wake of the HBOS scandal in early 2008, when the bank's share price fell by 20 per cent following carefully planted rumours that it was in trouble, Jonathon Crook of law firm Eversheds was scathing in his attack on the authorities: 'The effectiveness of the FSA as a prosecutor remains questionable. While it has had some success on relatively straightforward cases, it has yet to prove its mettle on a major matter.'

The HBOS incident was seized on by an indignant press, despite the events being no different from what is rumoured to occur on an almost daily basis in company shares spanning the length and breadth of the stock market. Rumours began circulating one morning that banking giant HBOS was in financial dire straits, and – in the climate of fear that was gripping the markets at the time – the whispers were sufficient to cause a wave of panic selling, wiping a fifth off the share price. Whilst the fall was only temporary (they climbed off a low of 398p to end the day only 7 per cent down at 446.25), there was enough time for anyone involved in a 'trash and cash' conspiracy to make their money by shorting the stock. The FSA came out all guns blazing after the episode, promising to swiftly bring the culprits to justice, but a few months later admitted defeat in its hunt for the offenders, saying that no prosecutions would be forthcoming despite their investigations.

According to Roy Cutts, the criminals get away with their actions, because the FSA 'can't catch them'. However, he concedes that the FSA certainly has the technological abilities and manpower to make serious inroads in chasing up suspicious share price moves. Computer models that can spot anomalous trading patterns aren't just restricted to hedge-fund back-room boys trying to spot the next buy or sell signal for their traders.

'The FSA have got them,' he remarks. 'To me it should be relatively simple, because, if you see a pattern, if let's say a broker dealt before some important news came out and brokers B, C, D and F dealt as well, now if you see that pattern constantly, does that not ring bells?'

Steven Gold points to company announcements as being prime hunting ground for those seeking to make a quick turn front-running breaking news.

'It's all about takeovers. That's the key; or profit warnings. If people trade on the back of it from certain information, it's very hard to prove, certainly if it's a big stock – how many millions of shares trade in a day? So how much work would it be to go through all the trades looking for abnormal trades? Though if your normal trade size is 5,000 shares and all of a sudden you're doing 500,000 shares, that's going to set alarm bells ringing.'

The futures market is not immune from market abuse either, according to Damien Walsh, but the nature of the beast is less along the lines of insider dealing. Instead, the practice centres around placing fictitious orders to try to drive the price of a future up or down, depending on the true position being taken by the traders concerned.

'There are instances in the markets of traders taking liberties. There was this guy called the Scalper, who used an enormous amount of size and then pulled it all of a sudden to create a falling price that he took advantage of,' he recalls. 'Now, because he was trading so much, Eurex [a major European derivatives exchange, on which the Scalper dealt] didn't pull him up on it, because they were earning so much money. Each time he put on a trade, he was earning them thirty grand or so in charges. They seem to have a different approach to the rules for people that are bringing the business.

'This has been going on for years. He's got a whole team now, and all they do is take a position for a second, so they're on the bid with massive size, say 3,000 lots. They're also on the offer and the bid is just slightly, slightly bigger, so they just keep selling. People keep buying off them, so by now they've sold a couple of thousand. They just keep on adding them in on this side and never adding them in on this side, making it too big for people to attack it – and then they suddenly fucking pull it. They're short of shit-loads. You know, 3,000 futures – suddenly they're two ticks onside because all the people who are buying them there are now trying to sell them two ticks lower, where they've got their bid. That's a complete manipulation of the market. But the [exchange] doesn't care, because they're making so much money from it. To me, that is an unfair treatment of the market using sheer money.'

Market abuse can only flourish unchecked in an environment where turning a blind eye becomes utterly commonplace and de rigueur. It is impossible to imagine an environment where traders, brokers and company officials alike can siphon off enormous sums of ill-gotten gains without raising eyebrows at some level or another; be it internal compliance at individual firms, amongst fellow traders in dealing rooms, or amongst company and private accountants auditing their clients' earnings and bank balances.

The embarrassingly low number of successful prosecutions of those flouting the rules does the City's image no favours, and – despite the shocking nature of some of the escapades described above – individual brokers and dealers spreading false rumours and tipping one another off about embargoed announcements is just the tip of the iceberg.

On an institutional level, the five-figure trading scams using dummy client accounts are magnified to a gargantuan proportion; pension funds and hedge funds front-running takeovers and market-moving news stories are, I am told, rumoured to account for some staggering profits (and, by extension, losses on the other side) being amassed on a near-daily basis. That their actions are then aped by unscrupulous characters lower down the food chain is hardly surprising, given the lawlessness that many feel abounds in the markets.

However, the unsavoury behaviour of an immoral few should not be allowed to tar the majority of those working within the Square Mile, the lion's share of whom have no connection to under-the-counter, illicit activity. With 1.3 million workers in London's financial sector, there will always be those for whom the opportunity to feather their nests with ill-gotten gains overrides any sense of morality or public duty. But their actions are not representative of the overall system. Instead, drawing attention to insider dealing, as well as the lackadaisical approach to it of the regulatory bodies overseeing the City, demonstrates just how dangerous such an opaque, otherworldy way of doing business can become when guided by the wrong hands.

5. Done and Dusted

The myth-making and distortion of reality surrounding the City can be neatly summed up by my two meetings with Nick Finegold, founder and chairman of Execution Limited. Our first encounter takes place in the ultra-trendy, ultra-exclusive Shoreditch House, a private members' club on the eastern edge of the Square Mile, after we are introduced by a mutual friend. The three of us dine in opulent luxury, six floors above ground in a roof-level restaurant with views over the lit-up City skyline. Waiters hover by our table like well-trained flies, diving in pre-emptively whenever a glass is near to being drained. Having offered to cover the cost of the meal, Finegold orders food and wine with casual abandon, the price list of scant interest to a man who has been extremely well rewarded during his long career in the City.

Having worked for Natwest for nine years on the sales side, before setting up Deutsche Bank's London operation as head of global sales trading, he struck out on his own in 2001, establishing Execution, an agency brokerage handling annual trading volume of tens of billions of pounds. From his confident demeanour, not to mention his expensive wardrobe and vintage timepiece, it is clear that he is entirely at home in such an environment, and the ensuing evening's entertainment does nothing to dispel the image.

He talks casually about Stevie Wonder performing in

front of a 180 people at a party he recently attended, with no acknowledgement of how detached such a situation is from the real world in which 99 per cent of the public dwell. When he accidentally spills a glass of red over our friend's thousand-pound Mulberry, he is as unperturbed as if he'd scuffed a pair of cheap trainers.

We decamp to the bar for post-prandial single malts, as Finegold continues to regale us with tales straight out of the pages of *Hello!* magazine. By the time we part company, his driver waiting outside to whisk him back to his 250-acre farm in Kent, I would be forgiven for thinking that he typifies the stereotypical cashed-up City trader without a care beyond the Square Mile-sized ecosystem, the type the press likes to portray as inhabiting a galaxy far removed from planet earth. However, the truth is far stranger than the fiction, as is immediately evident the next time we meet, a week later, in his firm's extravagant dealing room.

Yes, he's done very well out of his sojourn in the City, but just as he's the first to admit he's been dealt a particularly generous hand in the game of life, he's equally quick to make sure that others benefit from his good fortune. Those on the receiving end of his largesse are not just those in his immediate vicinity – although, judging from the extraordinary design of Execution's offices, those working for him have not done badly out of the arrangement. The two trading floors are lit up in pink and mauve lights, with tropical fish tanks lining the far wall, and a miniature golf course running down the middle of the room. A projector beams last night's football – Scotland against Argentina – on to a vast wall at the other end of the rows of desks, in front of plush couches where traders are encouraged to take a break from the stress of dealing. A huge bowl of pick and mix sweets is on display, and, despite what has been a nightmarish day on the markets – 'like a seal clubbing', according to Finegold – the mood in the office is far from tense.

I arrive towards the end of Execution's seventh annual charity trading day, an initiative he introduced along with Execution's CEO, James Blackburn. The gross proceeds of all commission revenues made during the course of the day are converted to charitable funds and distributed by the Execution Charitable Trust, which, to date, has raised almost £6 million for philanthropic causes.

'The thing about charity trading day is that it's sustainable,' says Finegold. 'People take stuff that they were going to do anyway and divert more trades to us that day, allowing us to raise more money for charity. It was something that we all felt strongly about, and we wanted there to be a purpose to come to work, other than making money.'

Blackburn agrees, stressing that not only do Execution's employees have no problem foregoing their day's earnings in order to raise funds for charity, but their peers in the City feel the same way.

'We're supported unconditionally on our charitable trading days by our clients. Our business goes up five or six times on charitable trading day versus any other day, which implies that people are inherently charitable, and that therefore, if you provide them with a mechanism by which they can give, then inherently that is something that they want to do.'

The sustainability is based on the way clients can swell the charitable trust's coffers simply by doing their jobs the same way as the rest of the year, says Blackburn.

'If you can find a mechanism by which people can do something that they do every day, and at the same time be very charitable, I have no doubt that people will do business with you on that day. If they can do the same with you versus someone else, and it doesn't cost them anything, and at the same time someone benefits, they will do business with you instead.'

The principal beneficiaries are charities right across Britain and beyond. Three-quarters of the cash is distributed by the trust, of which Blackburn is chairman, while the remaining funds go to ARK, the international children's charity.

'We didn't want to just fund on our own doorstep,' he says. 'We wanted to spread our wings. We really set out on a mission to fund the length and breadth of the UK, and we've achieved that. We've funded Belfast, Glasgow, Edinburgh, Yorkshire, Manchester, Exeter, Wales . . . We have funded thirty charitable causes now, and we have a core of about twenty. We are an entrepreneurial company, and we want to be entrepreneurial in our giving.'

Despite public perception about 'greedy' bankers and uncaring, unfeeling financiers, Finegold asserts that 'the City is packed full of philanthropists, people that are incredibly generous. I think it may have a PR issue, in that people tend to [give to charity] privately rather than publicly, but charity trading days here and at places like ICAP have been around for a long time. This is our seventh year, so it's not a reaction to the current environment.'

Blackburn points out that several other firms also run similar charity trading days, something he feels is of even greater importance during the latest economic downturn.

'We're going into a time right now in which, arguably, raising charitable money either from statutory funding or from high-net-worth individuals or from [other] individuals, will become increasingly difficult,' he comments.

'Yet the demands on the community projects that we support – as more people become unemployed – get higher and higher, so there's an inverse correlation between the money they get and the services they're asked to provide. So for me, at times like this, the charity work that we do is worth three times as much as it is in other times, regardless of how much we raise.'

The proceeds of this year's event are in the region of £650,000, down from the £1.5 million raised in 2007, reflecting the general slowdown in institutional dealing and trading volumes during the credit crisis slump.

Steven Gold is also vocal in his assertion that whilst the benevolent side of the City might not attract much attention, it thrives all the same.

'People don't know that a lot of people in the City donate a lot of money to charity,' he remarks. 'I've been to lots of events where there's been some pretty serious money.'

Gold also sees the fact that his salary means his wife doesn't have to earn money as means to an ends, since it allows her to volunteer in the charitable sector.

'She's a charity worker. I earn the money, I make rich people richer, and she's my moral yardstick, because she's doing good work for charity. She doesn't need to work – I earn all the money and I feed my son and I look after her, make sure she gets everything that she needs to run the house, so she can go out and do some charity work and can earn nothing to do it.'

Of course, all this can't be denoted in binary code (0 = the City is a modern-day Gomorrah, 1 = it's a Utopian charity-funding wonderland). Instead, the sheer diversity of the attitudes and ways of life on display means the City deserves to be viewed in the same shades of grey as the rest of society, rather than presumed black until proven to be white. There is plenty of greed; drink and drugs abound; and so on – but it is just not good enough to be blinded to the rest of the City by the light shone off those at the extreme, unpalatable end of the scale.

The 1980s 'greed is good' stereotype of Gordon Gekko rapacity still exists, along with all of the related macho posturing, which manifests itself in a myriad of forms – racism, sexism, homophobia and elitism, for example – although in many firms the breed is becoming extinct, as sales trader Paul O'Connor notes.

'I think with time going on, and the fact that they are recruiting more graduates – plus the fact that the younger generation are definitely more liberal – the City is correcting itself.'

However, earlier in his trading career, the homophobia he experienced at the hands of fellow traders went unpunished by his superiors.

'They let a lot go unchecked, whether it's knowing the people working for them have got drink or drug problems, whether knowing the people working for them are sexist, homophobic or racist. They know it and they don't address it – as long as the person is giving their pound of flesh and working and making them money and doing their job. The whole diversity programmes that all the banks run – it's all lip service. They don't give a shit if there's homophobia and racism on their trading floors.

'I used to hear homophobia constantly. I think it was one of those situations where people knew I was gay, but it was unsaid, because I hadn't come out. But it didn't stop them from being homophobic in my vicinity, bosses of mine as well. And even racism wasn't exactly covered up, and sexism . . . As long as we got results, as long as we got our commission and good feedback from our clients, they didn't really give a shit.'

O'Connor says that this uncaring stance extends to the health of individual traders as well, with employers more interested in the firm's balance sheets than the physical wellbeing of their workers.

'I think the banks know the situation, and they don't do random drugs tests, because they know half their staff would be on it, and they know that in a high-pressure job they have to allow their traders to have these excesses. They don't care about the health of their workforce as long as they're making money.'

Over in Canary Wharf, the heat in the cauldron of the trading room is markedly less intense than it used to be, says Jonny White.

'There's no bullying now,' he maintains. 'You're not allowed to now. You just can't do it. There are ageism and diversity [policies], which means they can't call me "fucking Jew", but they still do. They don't take the piss as much because there are five Jews out of twenty in our section, so we arm ourselves. Ninety-nine per cent of Jews in the City who work for the bigger places have a case for discrimination, but they choose not to follow it up. Because number one, you've got to know you're gonna win. Number two, your career's fucked the minute you do it.'

The women with whom he works don't suffer fools gladly, having learned how to fend for themselves along with the other minorities in the dealing room.

'Women brokers and traders hold their own better than most guys in my view,' he says.

It's the same in the Israeli army, I tell him, where girls

in border police units often try to act more male than the men to show their mettle.

'Yeah – geezer birds,' says Jonny in response, before moving on at Gatling-gun speed to sum up the average prop trader for me. 'To be a pure driven trader you've gotta have balls of steel, a stinking horrible personality and be a nasty person, a risk taker and a gambler. There are very few out there who are the nicest people in the world and are good traders.'

However, despite having to be gamblers at heart – 'a gambling mentality is in you inherently' – he says that traders have to also be 'highly disciplined, because you're watched every minute of every day. Your boss knows what you're doing, how much you're making, and there are risk management programmes. Gone are the Nick Leeson days where he did what he wanted, booked it to an account, and nobody would look. You just can't do that any more.'

'Any more' was becoming a catch phrase of my interviews – the City's transformation into a more modern, self-aware entity was entirely in line with that of the rest of society's progression as the world gets wiser. Futures trader Damien Walsh also demarcates between the 'then' and 'now' camps.

'Now it's a very different game to what it used to be. Because there used to be a lot more people making more money than normal people were. Now, there are a lot of people making decent money in a lot of industries, and there are a lot fewer traders making amazing, amazing money. So, that combined means that traders are generally a lot more careful now.'

This caution dictates traders' out-of-hours behaviour as well, Walsh says.

'I find that most traders' excesses are quite minor rebellions. They're like a big fucking weekend out with the boys, or a splashed-out holiday, rather than constant excess.'

Walsh also draws a distinction between traders and brokers, repeatedly ramming home what he sees as a fundamental difference between the two species' habits and customs.

'Unless a trader was going out for lunch for a special occasion, they'd be eating salads from Marks and Spencer,' he says. 'The brokers, however: fucking sushi every day followed by caviar. That's the difference. Traders aren't like that. Traders have to be so smart. Brokers can be complete morons and just act like the nicest guy on earth. Just like a guy I went to school with who is now broking. He was never a good student; I bet he never, ever quotes a number without looking at a calculator first, but he is such a smooth talker. Now, the only pressure he's got is maintaining being a smooth talker. He's never got to worry about what the market's doing.'

According to Walsh, 'a broker's excesses are because he's a wealthy guy and flamboyance is going to be in their nature. I think a trader's excesses are venting. I think there is such a build-up of stress and pressure that they are just trying to get off. I speak to brokers all the time. I never hear a broker pissed off. Never. Even in all this time when everyone's getting stopped out every five seconds. No broker I hear is miserable. You speak to traders, and any day of the week they can be having a fucking nightmare and they won't answer your call. And so the traders' excesses might, you know, blow out all the others', but that's not the people you hear about.'

At this point, Walsh launches into a stream of invective

against the media, castigating it for singling out traders as poster boys for the excess that he says is prevalent across society.

'I mean, everyone knows how rich Bill Gates is, but they don't say, "Oh, fucking software designers, man. Fucking software designers take all that money. All I want to do is send an e-mail and they're just living on a fucking 200-metre yacht." What's the difference? What about private doctors?'

There is not enough time in a trader's life to get up to even a tenth of the hedonistic activities that the public imagines them to, he assures me.

'I mean, I heard a lot about the hard living happening previously, but the nature of electronic trading has changed that a lot. Because it used to be that you'd be trading from 8.30 a.m. till 4.30 p.m., maybe an hour later for Europe, and then you were done. And all that stress was compacted into nine, ten hours. Now the minimum any trader [here] works is twelve, thirteen hours mostly. You start at seven in the morning, you finish at seven at night, and there's only so much partying you can fit in. It's a time when drugs are seen in a very different light to the eighties and nineties. and I just don't think it's very relevant any more.'

His day-to-day routine makes for sobering reading, especially for anyone who thinks traders have an easy ride in their pursuit of wealth.

'You trade for twelve hours non-stop. Maybe taking a piss every few hours. Maybe getting lunch, although if it's busy you'll be sending out one of the work-experience guys to get it for you, and if you do go out you're fucking running because if you miss something you're going to kill yourself. And you're talking [constantly], and on top of that now we've got all these "squawk" services, so you get all the news that's coming in over a Tannoy, but you can't really understand the implications of a news story just from a few words. You don't know anything. There are TVs on everywhere so that you can try and sneak a glimpse, but you're basically just staring at these numbers, and the best indicator you can get is watching what the markets are actually doing.

'People deal with the stress by doing as much as they can to make money. Because the more money you make, the less money you have to make before you're happy – not that you are ever happy. And that's the other big thing. The bad days are fucking awful. The really bad days you're fucking suicidal. You know, you won't go in for a couple of days, you'll go out and spend some money. Just do something. You literally punch the wall. Especially if it's not your fault. If the system goes down it's even worse. But a good day is never that good. You lose fifty grand, it's the worst day you ever had. Make fifty grand – maybe I should have made 100. Whatever happens, because the pressure is on so much to outperform your own expectations and the expectations of the people you're working for, you're never going to quite be doing well enough.'

His depiction of trench-like conditions reminds me of Lyon's and Cutts's old trading stories, except Walsh's version is more sombre.

'You're really in the thick of it, you're fighting against the big boys, and you're fighting against every other fucking trader. It's like a battle front. And you get pretty close to the boys around you. You know, you spend twelve hours a day with them. And you learn a lot about them, and you'll help them out whenever you can.

Whenever you've got a chance. So there's a definite camaraderie,' he ends, on a more positive note.

Given the pressure of this environment, it is perhaps understandable – though not excusable – to hear how Walsh reached conclusions about women in the workplace.

'Where I used to work, they tried very regularly to get in women to be traders. Eventually they managed to convince a girl that worked in the back office to start being a trader, and after two weeks she just disappeared and then sent in a letter saying she had to leave due to stress. I know another girl that was a trader, and she moved into broking, and those are the only two that I've ever come across. The firm that I work in now has got women working there – not as traders, but they work in the room, so it's not like the environment is too sexist. You can't be an idiot if you're going to be a trader. You can be an arsehole but you can't be a fucking idiot. And if you pull some shit, I promise you because of the reputation, bosses in financial companies are so much more wary of stepping over lines like sexism and political correctness than most other industries. The thing is about trading, you need to be fucking tough, and I found in the workplace that when things go wrong, women need to talk about them a lot more and – right or wrong, sexist or not – there's no room for it in trading. You need to be on the fucking screens. And stop your fucking moaning, you know? That's the bottom line.'

Walsh is right to distinguish between traders and brokers when it comes to the way in which they spend their working day. I feel a mixture of envy and pity for his routine, part of me wishing that I had been unleashed on the markets not on behalf of my clients, but purely for my own book, my P+L figures sending me from hero to zero and back again countless times over the course of a single day.

At the same time, the idea of being so restricted in my movements is not something I would have been able to put up with for long – though that's not to say I was as footloose and fancy free as those brokers who specialized in long-term investing. What I experienced, instead, was a hybrid form of both worlds; able to sit back and take it easy at times (at least, once my apprenticeship was over at my first firm), at others hunched over the screens and caught up in a whirlwind of frenzied activity when my trading clients wanted to get a piece of the action.

During those periods, I couldn't leave the desk for even the most hastily smoked of cigarettes; my role was simply to concentrate with a cultish zeal on the gyrations of whatever stock we were trading. During more relaxed spells, however, when I had no live short-term positions or the markets were going through a lethargic patch, there was nothing stopping me whiling away entire days in frivolous fashion: buying a hundred scratch cards and spending the post-lunch lull scraping them with pound coins, or betting on everything from the day's horse racing to who could name every component of the FTSE100 without looking. Our bosses took things even more easily, thinking nothing of taking two- or three-hour lunches deep in City watering holes below street level, where lack of mobile phone signals meant they could drink the day away without being disturbed by colleagues or clients.

Steven Gold appreciates that side of his work.

'It's fun in the City. Can you sit in an accountant's

office and – because it's a quiet day – talk about football for two hours with your colleagues?'

While he accepts that there is a tendency for some in the City to live up to the type of excesses Damien Walsh describes, he doesn't subscribe to that way of life.

'I never did that. I've never been flash in terms of spending outwardly or showing it with clothes and jewellery. It's just not me. What I spend all my money on is really lovely holidays, five-star hotels. Plus I'm on my third Porsche.' He hastily adds: 'That's the only one thing in my life that's outwardly flash, the Porsche; but I didn't buy it to be flash. It's because I like the car. I could afford it. That's just the way it is – that's what I like.'

Walsh is keen to dispel the suggestion that the City is awash with Class As, echoing Damien's position that only those without sin should be casting the first stone.

'I haven't seen drugs. Drink? Yeah, people drink a lot in the City, but people drink a lot in the advertising industry. People drink a fair amount, though less now at lunchtimes, because there's too much pressure on jobs.'

Hedge-fund manager Rob Davis sums up very succinctly his own approach to the excesses.

'You might still find that on the investment bank trading floors; some of the market makers might be doing drugs. But at a hedge fund it's a proper West End, Mayfair-type business'.

The same goes for Jonny White.

'Sometimes I'll have a joint, but ... [the image of a drug-fuelled financial sector] has changed. It used to be like that ten, twenty years ago, when it was like that across the board. Especially when the LIFFE floor was about, it was very prevalent. But I've never done it in my life, it's not the way I was brought up, plus I'm not stupid.'

Others weren't as self-regulating, he says.

'It's the herd mentality. But, slowly over the last five to ten years, that has floored. They've put a lid on it, with internal random drug tests.' But he qualifies this: 'If you're making two, three, four million a year for the company and come back pissed from lunch, the boss will turn a blind eye, because you're doing well. He doesn't want you to go and work for someone else, so he turns a blind eye.'

He believes that perception is unfairly skewed because of the media frenzy during bonus season – though he accepts it's smoke that wouldn't exist without the underlying fire.

'The public resents seeing the greed thrown in their faces, seeing people going out to bars at this time. When it comes to bonus time, people go out and spend it on champagne, Porsches, houses in town, holidays – but these guys are making money. I mean, what's the matter with being flash?'

He has no problem with the setup himself.

'I'm in it and I wanna make as much money as possible, but I'm not flash. The City's changed from what it used to be, especially over the past year and a half. We're doing a job the same as anyone else; we're trying to create wealth for everybody. If I bring in more clients, I get paid more, the bank gets more money, the bank will invest more money, and give more people jobs . . .

'We're doing the same as everyone else but we're in the spotlight more, because we earn more money doing it. The people that look at the City and go, "Oh, these fucking wankers, earning all this money," they're just jealous. And the people that write about it can go fuck 'emselves – try it. The man in the street that says, "Oh, these fucking traders," and everything – who is he? If he's gonna sit there and say, "Look at these flash wank-ers," we could turn round and say, "What about you, you poor little git?" Why can't we say that? Because he hasn't got his arse into the kind of jobs we have, so he's jealous. What about the guy that's going out and selling tables, and he's a very successful seller of tables so he's earning himself 300 grand a year. Who's having a go at him? No one. He's working hard, and that's what we're trying to do too.'

It's inevitable that working hard leads to playing even harder, says Darren Carver.

'Everyone needs an excuse to unwind; we're in a high-pressured job. It's quite a seductive environment to work in; for anyone looking for a quick fix, there's no better place than the City, because fortunes are won and lost on the press of a button. If you've got a gambling habit, there's no better place to do it than the City, espe-cially with someone else's money. If you've got a drink-ing habit, there's no better place to do it than the City, because you blend into a crowd – it goes largely unno-ticed, and it seems to be accepted.'

While some people might be encouraged to develop an excessive streak upon entering the City, it is an innate part of others' personalities from childhood, he says, meaning that they naturally gravitate towards the City, where they can let their inner hedonist run riot.

'I think some people fall into it. I think that for a person with an addictive nature, this is the place to be – but it doesn't necessarily follow that everyone that works in the City has got an addictive nature. There are some very clever people up here who are making some serious money. But at the same time they've all lost money together.'

It is the dichotomy in his last statement that best sums

up the myth-making about the Square Mile. Just as fortunes are won every day in the market, there are those nursing their wounds on a daily basis – but they're not the ones on whom the media tend to focus.

Similarly, stories of drug-addled traders hurling themselves from the nineteenth floor of central London hotels make for great copy but does little to paint a true picture of everyday life in the City. The real question that honest observers ought to be asking is whether brokers and traders really are more prone to excess than the man on the street, or is the stereotyping simply another way for outsiders to delegitimize City workers and cast them as pantomime villains?

6. The Making of Monsters

Towards the end of my lunch with Rob Davis, once he's spelled out the trials and tribulations in the life of a hedge-fund manager, I try to inject a dose of reality.

'You and I have got more money than 95 per cent of people who live in the same country as us,' I say. 'It's just that we're surrounded by other people in the same position, so we lose touch with the world outside our bubble. We're divorced from reality. I paid cash for my house in Jerusalem, which is unthinkable for most of my peers in Israel, let alone those lower down the scale.'

Rob nods in agreement, as waiters sweep away the crumbs from the remains of our meal.

'It's nuts,' he replies. 'I own property in the East End, residential properties. I was there the other week, and there's literally about seven people living in one house. You think to yourself, what have I got to worry about in life? But it's just the greed in the City that does it to you.'

I was hooked from the moment I was unleashed into the City, and it's no wonder that others succumb to the heady concoction of fast cars, pretty girls and even prettier drugs. The extravagant architecture and pristine condition of the Square Mile itself, as well as Canary Wharf, and – for the hedge-fund community – Mayfair and the West End, only adds to the sense of otherworldliness.

The City is an oasis of bright lights, bordered by far less salubrious surroundings. A five-minute stroll past the borders of the Square Mile reveals the harsh truth for those on the wrong side of the tracks. The long rows of dilapidated East End council flats have more in common with the gritty reality of Richard Billingham photographs than any of the gleaming office blocks with which they share a postcode. Inside the City, however, there is an air of surrealism, akin to a Vegas casino, where clocks, windows and any other objects that remind gamblers of the world outside are eschewed in favour of bright lights and spinning wheels.

The myth that London's streets are paved with gold is not to be spoiled by having to encounter the less fortunate a mere stone's throw away from the pristine City streets. Even the designers of Shoreditch House play their part in the cover-up, its wall-to-ceiling restaurant windows offering breathtaking views over the City skyline not extended round the whole building, to avoid taking in the less attractive vista to the East of the club.

It's the same story in Canary Wharf. Once cosily ensconced inside the realm of moneyed skyscrapers and upmarket bars and restaurants, it is easy to forget that on the other side of the divide dwell real people. Looking out from the Docklands Light Railway, bleak and forbidding estates huddle between expanses of wasteland; urban decay and an air of gloom hanging over the roofs in stark contrast to the 'sky's the limit' atmosphere amongst the Canary Wharf elite. One of the clearest signs of this division in London – a capital city that ostensibly strives to be a seven-million strong melting pot – can be found along the main roads of respective communities.

In Canary Wharf, a high-tech, dot-matrix system flashes from on high the latest index movements and foreign exchange rates to pedestrians walking below, the level of the FTSE and the dollar/yen rate deemed the most important figures to drum into our consciousness. Further up the Jubilee Line in Kilburn, the fluctuations of the money markets take a back seat. There residents are encouraged to concentrate instead on a different set of figures: 'Crime down 21% in Brent,' boast advertising hoardings.

Along Cork Street, the art-lover's Mecca in the heart of the West End, three tourists act out a bizarre ritual. Spotting a sparkling Lamborghini Countach parked by the side of the road, two of the beaming trio strike pop-star poses alongside it, and the third takes their photo. Seeing a new F1 McLaren further up the street, they dash off to repeat the trick, the baubles of the über-rich having become modern-day Nelson's Columns to this generation of day-trippers.

They can hardly be blamed, since today's cash- and celebrity-worshipping culture plays no small part in elevating the trappings of wealth to the level of artistic achievement or academic prowess. Magazines fawn over millionaires as though simply the amassing of fortunes is enough to set apart the individuals concerned from the rest of humanity, and their admirers bestow upon them the status of instant deities. I don't plead entirely innocent to the charges myself, though I like to think I'm a far cry now from how I used to be when offering sacrifices at the altar of Mammon during my City days.

However, even back then I was regularly appalled at the lengths to which the City drove some people to rewrite their own rulebooks, slashing and burning normal codes of behaviour and replacing them with severely twisted versions. During my first year on the dealing floor, I felt a hand on my shoulder one dress-down Friday morning, as the collar of my sweater was wrenched down to check the label I was wearing. 'Good – it's Gucci,' said my faceless assailant, before I spun on my heel to discover his identity. It was one of the other juniors.

His Stalinesque spot–check of my clothing still stands out as testament to how quickly, and how deeply, rookies in the business get bitten by the City bug; and, once infected, the only way is down. Cash rules everything around you once your world is framed by the market's borders: not only is your whole raison d'être simply dealing with money and trying to make more of it for both you and your clients, but also the way to define your sense of self-worth and importance is graded solely in financial terms.

'Money is the only true measure of performance, the only way that investment banks express their gratitude,' says an unnamed banker in *City State*, a study of the London financial markets published in 2001, whilst the authors themselves take the following view of society as a whole: 'Guilt about money is little more than a quaint memory from a repressed age – this may or may not be a good thing, but at least we have shed our oldest vice: hypocrisy.'

It's misleading to single out the City as the disease itself, rather than a symptom of a worldwide malaise. But at the same time the City is notorious for bringing out the worst in its charges.

'When I was buying Invensys for clients, I'd do it in lots of twenty grand at a time,' remembers Rob Davis. 'Now, in my fund, I buy twenty million Invensys at once. That's the size I have to deal in now. I think about how fortunate I am – I feel like a bit of a player sometimes, dealing in that size.'

Feeling like a 'player' was what seduced Steven Gold, whose initial awe at his superiors' dealing in '$50 million

of Reuters shares' propelled him to pursue a lifelong
career doing likewise.

There's a similar story from Paul O'Connor, who
speaks about nine-figure trades with a nonchalance
belying the enormity of what he once carried out on a
daily basis.

'Yeah, I used to do £100 million deals,' he shrugs.

The numbers involved did have an influence on his
sense of self-worth, he admits.

'It's elitism, I think,' he remarks. 'I thought that I was
better than a private client broker [because of it].'

However, he maintains that he wasn't enslaved to the
concept of more money equalling more respect, at least
not when it came to those above him in the pecking
order.

'The people that I looked up to, and this is just me,
were people whose intellect I respected. I worked with
very few people in my career – no more than five – who
I respected intellectually; their approach to markets and
trading, and their intellectual approach. That's who I
looked up to, and it was nothing to do with money. But,
saying that, the people who are treated god-like in the
City are people like hedge-fund gurus, the people who
have literally banked themselves £200–300 million. They
have private jets, huge net worths, and command a huge
amount of power – because when you are head of a
company like that, you have a thousand brokers all chasing your commission.'

Despite Daniel Barnes's childhood desire to make
money at all costs, it was a healthy, pre-City exposure to
the real world that helped shape his attitude to the life he
was about to enter.

'I was going out with a Latvian stripper when I first

started working in the stock market,' he begins. 'She used to work in Browns, and she was the complete contrast from me – I don't mean to sound snobbish about strippers, but their view on life can be very simple. It's like, "Who cares if someone sees my body? We're here to make money, there are a whole bunch of guys who want to pay for services, and we're very happy to provide it, so we'll just do it." For me that was a social taboo, and yet it all made sense. So I think I went into the City without being judgemental, because it was a case of all these bankers doing things because they provided a service. I was philosophical about it. There weren't any ethical issues – it was just "We're here to do business."'

He argues that his – and others' – decision to opt for money over morals in certain situations cannot be blamed on being 'blinded' by the riches on offer. It's far more calculating than that, and that anyone choosing to go into the City does so under the knowledge that their ethics may well get compromised along the way. He cites some Brazilian exploits to prove the point.

'When I went to Latin America, it wasn't the case that I just turned up in São Paulo and found myself a brothel. A month before I went, I told a buddy of mine I was going, and his Brazilian contact sent me an e-mail with a description of how the best brothel works. I had a whole month to think about it and I still went and did it.'

This decoupling of his own desires from a more conventional set of guidelines spilled over into his work, and was more than encouraged by his superiors, with disastrous consequences for the world at large. Barnes was right at the heart of the creation of one of the debt-laden financial instruments that has since been blamed for causing the credit crunch: Collateralized Debt Obligations (CDOs).

'At my bank I was sitting there syndicating CDOs,' he recalls. 'These CDOs basically had mortgage-backed securities in them, and every time we did a CDO we made eight or nine million dollars of fees. We were a structuring and marketing desk, so we would simply create them and then try to sell them off; our upside was the fees, and there was no trading risk, since we had nothing left on the books. If there were no buyers on the other side, then that business wouldn't have existed, but the buyers that we were creating were other CDOs who, alongside investing in mortgage-backed securities, were then buying into CDOs. So you had CDOs buying into CDOs which were buying into more CDOs, and so on.

'When I first joined, I said to the guy I was working with, "This seems a bit fucked up, doesn't it? We're creating something so that we can take fees out of it, which is then being bought by another CDO . . . we're kind of part of this whole vicious circle that's going around." He said, "Look, I agree with you, but we're not paid to think like that – we're paid to make money. And if it becomes a problem then we'll deal with it." And that was the end of the conversation.'

Barnes didn't stop worrying about what kind of monster they were helping to create, but at the same time did nothing more to try to apply the brakes to the process.

'It lingered in my mind that this thing could turn out to be ugly, because it looked like a true bubble. If things are just growing on their own back, it's a self fulfilling prophecy, and that's what these so-called ABS CDOs were. They were buying into other ABS CDOs which were buying into other ABS CDOs. It didn't seem right – it seemed like the market could be lining itself up for a big fucking collapse. However, when it's not just you but the whole firm and it's the entire industry, plus there's a massive sociological phenomenon which is occurring on the back of that – i.e. people being able to buy houses for the first time that they never could before – then no one person can just sit there and go, "Hey, hold on a second guys, this is all entirely wrong."'

I draw a contrast between his refusal to swim against the clearly corrupt tide with Rosa Parks's determination to right the racist wrongs in her society. But he rejects this.

'The difference in the analogy is that, yeah, you are on the bus and you're trying to get yourself sat further forward, but here it was a case of well, "Am I even going to be on the bus at all?" I mean, there wasn't even a debate – it would still go on without me: "If you're not gonna do it, well there's some other guy who would be happily paid half a million dollars to do this instead."'

Given that line of reasoning, was it therefore worth continuing to work in something he believed to be immoral, just because he thought that, if someone was going to profit from it anyway, it might as well be him? The 'only following orders' defence is alarming to hear, yet appears to have salved Barnes's conscience, despite the bloody consequences of the credit bubble's eventual bursting.

'Did I think I was right in just letting it be, just accepting it and going along for the ride? No. But would I have done any differently if I had my time again? No.'

Staying on the 'ends justifies the means' theme, I paint a hypothetical scenario to see quite how far Barnes would be prepared to go in pursuit of power and influence.

'Take an Afghan farmer who says, "I want to make a difference in the world," but all he can do is raise his goats and sheep and just provide for his family. He's never going to become, as you put it, important, or have a rank, since he's just living hand to mouth. You tell him that if he grows poppies that will be turned into heroin, then he can make a fortune and can garner influence and go into politics and have a massive influence in his world. Knowing that the heroin will be sold to addicts around the world, sowing death and misery at the same time, should he do it?'

To Barnes, the answer is simple.

'Quite frankly I think, yeah, that guy should go and grow poppies, sell heroin, whatever. Because if he doesn't do it, someone else will, so better that he does it, because at least he has the right intentions.

'Bringing it back into the context of the financial world, the market is a web of thousands and thousands of roles and functions that all come together to create the market that we live in. If you look back into history, the financial markets have been the cornerstone of every period of prosperity, and with prosperity comes a lot of benefits that people quickly forget. If you look at what the last seven years did for the credit markets, the bubble facilitated things that people never could have had before. Compared to two years ago we may be in a worse situation, but compared to eight years ago there are a bunch of people who have home ownership which they always dreamed of – which in their little world means a lot. Yeah, some of them will lose their homes, but a lot of them won't.

'We can question the fundamentals of whether the credit bubble was right or wrong, but it did facilitate that. We can look at the CDO situation and say, "You could have rung the alarm bells." Yeah, I could have, but the argument could be flipped: if we weren't in the credit crunch you may have asked: "How can you be justified in bringing to a halt the very thing that was making a lot of people feel more prosperous?"'

Of course, this view is based on the idea that home ownership is a cornerstone of progress. It would be a different story on a kibbutz, the classic socialist experiment, where people couldn't care less about owning a home; instead taking their comfort from knowing there is a safety net beneath them more reliable than any welfare state. However, given that the West is still avowedly capitalist, Barnes's argument is steeped in the same money-hungry soil of which the rest of our society is made up.

'A lot of this ultimately stemmed from the States,' he says. 'Fannie Mae was set up by Roosevelt at the end of the Great Depression, because he wanted to get the housing market up and running again. To do that, people needed mortgages, and it was a question of "How is this mortgage market ever going to be funded – who is going to make loans to homeowners?" So what Fannie Mae did was take the risk of the mortgages, meaning that all these banks could go and sell mortgages, but could then sell them on to Fannie Mae, so that effectively Fannie was funding those mortgages.

'That was part of Roosevelt's plan to end the Great Depression, but fast forward to the late sixties and it was slightly redundant. Suddenly Fannie are funding people's mortgages but the market was by now up and running, so they decided to privatize the thing. And they created another company, Freddie Mac, which was created effectively just to give the notion that there was competition between the two. But to all intents and purposes, everyone always viewed the companies as being exactly the same, and everyone viewed the companies as being government agencies. Even if they were listed on the New York Stock Exchange and were actively traded, people just considered them to be government risk.

'Ideologically Fannie and Freddie were there to allow people to own homes, and in 1995 Fannie and Freddie were both allowed by the government to buy the mortgage-backed securities that were securitizing sub-prime mortgages. Prior to that, they had pretty strict lending criteria; pretty strict criteria as to the mortgages in which they could invest, but by investing in mortgaged-backed securities which had sub-prime mortgages underlying them, they were effectively funding the sub-prime market as well. Not on their own, but along with the rest of the market.

'According to rumours, even John Kerry [US Democratic presidential candidate] sent letters to Fannie pleading: "Hey, you should buy more, because this is bringing home ownership – not to the rich, but to a whole underclass of people that have never ever owned a home before, and it's a big thing. It's a really important thing for the development of society." So home ownership was embraced by people at the top. They played their part just as much in pushing for these things, which ultimately went on to create the credit crunch. In 2004 I think they were buying something like 40 or 45 per cent of all sub-prime mortgage-backed securities, which is a mammoth amount. I mean, these are two private companies which on the back of the government are being encouraged to buy, so they have a much greater impact. And, to be honest, if you'd interviewed anyone in 2005 and said, "Are these guys doing the right thing?", I think most people would have found it very hard to say no, they're doing the wrong thing. Everyone was encouraging everyone else.'

In the space of a few, impassioned minutes, Daniel has – at least in his eyes – adroitly demonstrated why blaming the banking system alone for the credit crisis is pure folly. I am inclined to agree, in a broad sense, since it is impossible to see how the entire non-City populace had willingly gone along for the greedy and avaricious ride without raising any objections if they really felt so misled. Whoever was happily buying into the capitalist system and benefiting from the freely available credit was, by definition, complicit on the way up – so it seems strange to pretend not to have sanctioned the bubble's formation in the first place.

Michael Parnes, as chief executive of a brokerage bucking the trend and expanding during a downturn, believes that getting to grips with the new reality is the only way his firm – and society as a whole – will come through the hard times. 'Now you've got to work much harder for your money,' he comments matter-of-factly.

'Our generation, and I speak for us as twenty-somethings, has lived on credit. Speaking for myself, I perhaps haven't lived within my means, and I'm not alone in that. I think we're going to return to times of frugality which would be our parents' or grandparents' generation, the forties and fifties, where they were careful with their money. They had to be. Whereas now, everything's just been merry: we had yuppies in the eighties, we've got credit booms and people getting easy credit and being dishonest in applications, and they're getting caught out, and we're all paying the price. I think the return to frugality is by design, it's not choice. There isn't the credit. Lots of my peers have lost their jobs, they can't get the credit, and now people have got to be very resourceful and very careful. We've had it good, we've had it easy – we're spoilt, and we're going to find it hard to swallow.'

A few years ago, riding the crest of the buoyant stock market, Parnes worked for another broking house, 'raising money for the crack cocaine of AIM brokers: IPOs [Initial Public Offerings: bringing companies to market and selling their shares to the public] in a bull market in 2002, when AIM had become very sexy and lucrative, and you could raise money and charge big fees for it, and people weren't that concerned with quality. They were just raising money blind, which is part of the reason that we see ourselves in a declining market at the moment.'

Now his role in the City sees him adopt a far more cautious stance in terms of who he deals with, in line with the wider industry's reluctance to grant cheap credit.

'We are a specialist stockbroker dealing for institutions and ultra-high-net-worth individuals only. We only deal for private clients who show a minimum net asset worth of thirty million US dollars.'

He hasn't foregone all of the trappings of the bull market, however.

'We have solid gold membership cards which I issue to some of our ultra-high-rolling clients who spend a lot of money with us,' he smiles.

Whilst Parnes has no problem admitting that he enjoys the finer things in life, he does not feel that the City has made him obsessed with money; rather, since the business revolves around money, he sees it as natural that money is uppermost in the minds of those working in the markets.

'This is our job – we're not art dealers who are passionate about art. The endgame is that you're dealing in vast quantities of money, and that's what you're paid in. It's not a reciprocal trade agreement here. The endgame is to have cash in your bank account because you've completed a successful transaction – so, sure, we're here for the money, and I enjoy it as well. The deal is exciting, but I'm certainly not addicted to it.'

Rob Davis is less comfortable with his position in society, recognizing that he has, in fact, become ensnared by the lifestyle to which he was originally drawn.

'I continuously say to my wife, "We live in this bubble, we live in this bubble." All I get once, twice a week from my missus, is "Oh, this one's buying clothes in this shop, that one's buying clothes in that shop . . ." I would like to get away from it. But my family are here. And that's the bottom line really. This is where my family are from, this is where my wife's family are from. This kind of area is all we know. I try and avoid it as much as I can, but it's difficult sometimes.

'Do I like it? No, I hate this bubble we live in, it's wrong. I just don't like this whole greed factor – that's what I don't like about the City. People are too greedy, and people need to wake up and smell it. I feel a bit trapped, because I'm not one who likes change. And I'm a proud person – what would my friends say? I could just turn around and say I'm not enjoying it any more, I'm fed up with it – and the first thing people would say is "You're giving up loads of money." That's what people would think straight away.'

His predicament, such as it is, embodies a wider malaise in which money is put above all else in society's league table. Similarly the metamorphosis of the market into the shape it takes today is broadly in synch with the rest of the world's evolution. The internet, amongst other things, has spearheaded a drive towards instant gratification – whether pornography, purchasing power or plain contact with each other. Globalization has torn down walls, and benefited those seeking to take the stock market to dizzy new heights of power and control. At the same time, the inexorable rise of the 'money never sleeps' brigade ensures that ever more pressure is applied on those members of society playing catch-up, who are led to believe that in cash lies the answer to all their prayers.

The new-found ability of traders to instantaneously deal in exotic products and commodities has not been without its dangers, as the credit crisis so woefully demonstrates. However, in the rush to condemn the banking system, people have lost sight of the fact that – ultimately – it is human behaviour that drives the market, as anywhere else, and the market madness did not emerge from a vacuum. The internet poker phenomenon, the national obsession with scratch cards and lottery tickets, the unhealthy compulsion to live on credit – whether via mortgages, credit cards or any other borrowing-based system – means that it was almost inevitable that the market would follow suit.

The signs have been there for decades: David Kyte, one of the top futures traders of his day, was at the vanguard of the post-Big Bang, yuppie-led eighties, and gave a revealing interview to the *Sunday Times* in 1987: 'I trade anything that moves. If I lose £10,000, there's plenty more where that came from; if I make ten thousand, it's not going to make such a great advance on my equity. I don't think of it as money any more, it's just points. If I'm up, it gives me more to play with . . .' That Kyte now donates huge sums to charity and still runs his own highly successful futures trading firm is testament to his personal determination, but does not detract from the significance of the ultra-detached soundbite he uttered all those years ago.

Psychoanalyst Coline Covington, who has treated many Square Mile employees, has seen first-hand the influence the City has on the mindsets of those working within it.

'There is a culture that I'm aware of in certain parts of the City, especially before the current crisis, where there was so much power and things were going so high that there was quite a divorce from reality. There was a tangible feeling that you could do anything you wanted to. And to be cautious and to question things – particularly what might be a bad deal – was unheard of.

'I've had patients in top positions who were worried about a deal, who didn't want to back it or wanted to kill investments in a company, and the pressure around them was not to do anything about that – not to say die, basically. Since the crisis I think a huge amount of reality has come in, but before that it was powerful and scary at times – you couldn't show any vulnerability.'

Certainly during my early years in the dealing room I was not encouraged to talk about anything more emotional than the latest Arsenal result or the varying chest sizes of women walking in the street below our window. Once our firm was taken over by a European bank, there was a drive by the new owners to bring more humane, enlightened attitudes into the dealing room, but the resistance of the old guard was strong, and their efforts fell on stony ground.

In the vacuum left by how much remained unsaid on the desks, I simply aped my bosses' more unsavoury habits in an effort to scale the ladder, despite my initial misgivings.

It wasn't long before I began to believe the hype, genuinely attaching more weight to how much money I was making and how fast, rather than to the relationships I formed or the way I came across to those outside market circles.

All of the ways in which my money could be spent seemed opportune, not because of the benefit I'd derive from what I actually bought, but rather as simply a way of displaying how much spare cash I had and how easy-come, easy-go my funds now were to me. I was no more of a clothes connoisseur than the next man, so why spend £350 on a Dior hoodie that I wore just twice, or £200 on a pointless Vuitton scarf, other than to boast about the extortionate price tags?

Fine food didn't turn me on like it would a true aficionado, but ostentatiously spending four figures on lunch did. The fact that I, and all my guests, were high as kites on coke most of the time that we ate at Michelin-starred restaurants made it even worse; our appetites suppressed and our tastebuds paralysed beneath a layer of permafrost, we might as well have just heated up fifty-pound notes and eaten them instead, for all the enjoyment we got from the food itself. Drinking Cristal like water was done solely to make us feel like pinstriped Puff Daddys, rather than out of any innate love for champagne, prestige cuvée or not.

Even coke itself morphed from being a drug I loved on its own merits to becoming simply a way to flash my money. Scoring half an ounce at a time made me look, and feel, like the devil-may-care young broker I aspired to be, embarrassing as that may seem to me now. Finishing the lot in a marathon session raised me on to an even loftier dais in my mind, propelling me on to even dizzier heights (or depths) of excess. When the KLF famously burned a million pounds in cash during my wide-eyed, teenage years, the event seared an indelible impression on my mind. To me, their actions epitomized the pinnacle of narcissistic largesse, whatever their true intentions, and I wanted a piece of the action. I got it, a few years later, albeit in scaled-down form.

Even though I thought I'd left it all behind me when I upped sticks and left for Israel, the ever-spreading vine of capitalistic avarice was never far behind. At times I have felt it wrap me again in its stranglehold, at others I watch the effect it has on even the most unlikely victims. Recently, on a night out in downtown Jerusalem, a friend turned to me and – after peering around nervously to check who else was listening – whispered in hushed tones: 'I tried f/x [foreign exchange trading] for the first time today.' His admission was akin to that of a teenager speaking of faltering steps into the murky world of heroin, and the hook of his chosen drug exerted no less acute a grip. 'I lost money,' he went on, 'but I think I know why. I'll be better at it the second time . . .' The signs suggest he is destined to become just another Mrs Watanabe, the collective nickname given to the legions of Japanese housewives who trade currencies online with their families' savings.

A love of gambling has ensnared thousands of punters across the UK, and millions across the world, to the point that people have begun to develop a quasi-religious conviction that they are almost owed a streak of luck on a regular basis, simply for taking part in the betting culture at all. The press plays no small part, trumpeting lottery and bingo winners as though their achievements equal scaling Everest or trekking to the North Pole, yet rarely – if ever – devoting space to the crippling, life-blood-sucking side of gambling, where people lose all they have and more, desperately pursuing instant fortunes.

Those who treat the Stock Exchange as an arena for making uninformed snap decisions – like it's a gentrified roulette wheel – are as guilty as anyone of losing touch with reality. The peak of the madness was back in the days of the internet bubble, when – from the *Mirror's* City Slickers column to the ostensibly more sensible broadsheet commentators – share tips were hurled on a daily basis with no more gravity attached than the experts' naps for the day's horseracing on the sports pages. Traders and brokers were, of course, sucked into the fray as well, suspending normal investment behaviour in favour of punting anything boasting a .com suffix with wanton abandon.

The highlight of the day was, for a time, not the CNBC market commentary or technical analysis slots, but rather the dumbed-down Channel 4 game show *Show Me the Money*. Brokers waited with bated breath for the day's tip to be announced, knowing that the surge of buying would send the stock through the roof. Those moments summed up the casino that the market represents to many people. The underlying stock meant very little when it came to short-term trading; all that mattered was the three-letter stock code, how much money was available to back it and how good one's timing was on the way in and out of the trade. Even now, thinking back to my best trades, all that matters to me is how much I made in how short a space of time; the business models of the companies I was trading as irrelevant as the hors d'oeuvres I ate at Nobu when coked up to the eyeballs.

The advent of online trading has opened up the markets to an even wider audience of gamblers, especially once leverage was added to the mix. For an initial outlay of a few thousand pounds, wannabe-traders could punt five-figure sums to their heart's contents, on anything in which the spread-betting firms were willing to make a market.

Throughout 2008 there was a London Underground advertising campaign run by Capital Spreads, the financial spread-betting firm. Their giant poster ads attempted to shame those not apparently clued-up enough to understand the implications of hypothetical scenarios. 'The Chinese wrap up mineral rights throughout West Africa,' one ad began. 'Do you a) get on the blower and order a 21, two 16s and some butterfly prawns; b) start buying copper and enjoy the ride.' A picture of a solitary, curled-up prawn accompanies the question, leaving the viewer to decide whether they want to remain a part of the uninformed, uninvolved hoi polloi or join the ever-swelling ranks of the day-trading masses and open an account.

The language employed speaks volumes about the way the spread-betting companies want people to view the markets. Referring jovially to an open position as a 'ride' conjures up images of a theme park, a highly inflammatory and dangerous way to paint the weighty world of commodities trading to an unwitting public. Yet the advertising authorities evidently have no issues with the campaign.

Potential punters would do better to spend half an hour a day watching analysts deconstructing share-price graphs on the business channels and learning the art of technical analysis, rather than falling back on the 'wing and a prayer' option of blindly buying on a tipster's say-so, or thinking they can beat the market based on no more than a fumbled gut feeling.

If that seems harsh, it's worth considering why vast

swathes of the public look on in stunned disbelief on the occasion a share price rises after the company issues a profits warning. So many factors go into the movement of a share price, yet plenty of observers still believe price moves to be simply a case of 'bad news = instant move down', and the converse for seemingly positive announcements.

The realms of foreign exchange and commodities trading were once the preserve of those with a real, commerce-related reason to trade in those markets – those seeking to hedge positions and keep their business running within budgetary constraints. That the door to the market has now been wrenched open and hordes of punters allowed to stream through on to the virtual trading floor signifies that the detachment from reality has spread far beyond simply those physically working within the Square Mile.

7. Axis of Evil

To the untrained eye, Evil Knievel's palatial residence didn't look like a conventional crack den: sumptuous antique furniture lining the living room, hundred-year-old tomes of English classics on oak bookshelves, opulent oil paintings bordered by gold-leaf frames. But the sophisticated decor did not indicate a general subtlety in the way Evil proved his omnipotence to the outside world.

Not for him the art of 'stealth wealth', a theory promoted by a small and dying breed of City aficionados. Rather, he knew that his reputation relied on him casting a larger-than-life shadow across the markets and racecourses where he plied his trade. Hence his propensity to lay million-pound trades with one hand whilst backing horses to the tune of fifty grand with the other, as he was now. Sitting at his bank of liquid crystal monitors, he'd barely turned to look at me in the half hour since I'd arrived.

Not that I cared. During my two years as his broker, I'd more than got used to his brusque demeanour. The language he used gave him away as coming from the highest breeding; the way he employed it revealed how deep into the market-trader mindset he'd willingly sunk. 'You will purchase the stock for me this instant,' he barked into the handset clamped to his left ear, 'since failure to do so will effect a slaughter amongst your flock of dealers.' Slamming down the phone, he exhaled sharply as his eyes continued their staccato dance across the screens, hunting for the next trade like a hawk sizing up prey in the fields below.

Handed his account, I swiftly realized it was a golden opportunity, and not simply in terms of the commission I'd earn from his trading largesse. In market terms, being so close to Evil – otherwise known as Simon Cawkwell – was akin to sitting at the feet of a Talmud sage. I lapped up the education he bestowed upon me and did everything I could to foster the relationship which developed between us.

It paid off in spades. I became a regular visitor to his Kensington house, where we would spend drunken afternoons betting on anything and everything under the sun. He would consume two bottles of wine over lunch, whilst I made discreet use of regular cigarette breaks to suppress my appetite and stoke my arrogance by imbibing line after line of coke. My bosses could hardly complain about my absence from the trading room when I was with one of our biggest clients, and thus I was free to unshackle myself from my dealing-room chains and wend my way to Evil's lair.

Our relationship continued in this fashion until I called time on my City career, opting to take the money and run (into the arms of Israel and the IDF). Absence made the heart grow fonder, and Evil regularly called to check up on his former broker; fascinated by the manner in which I'd downed my trading tools and picked up a machine gun instead. After I'd left the City, I felt there was always the air of a spurned lover about him when we spoke: not in the sense that I'd abandoned him personally, more that I'd turned my back on the world in which he dwelt.

I could feel it again now as I sat watching him trade. His casual asides to me between deals were laced with defensiveness, as though he were having to justify to a sceptic why he was trading at all. It dawned on me as the afternoon wore on that, in fact, he had read the situation perfectly in terms of my cynicism, and I decided to press him on what was really underlying his lust for lucre.

Here was a man with a multi-million-pound fortune, with a cast-iron reputation as one of the City's shrewdest and boldest traders, and every possible material possession he could wish for – so why was he still obsessively pursuing even more money?

'Simon,' I began, in what I sensed was a lull in his otherwise frantic session of dealing, 'if you suddenly made half a billion pounds tomorrow, what would you do the day after?'

Turning slowly in his chair, he fixed his eyes on me properly for the first time that day, an expression of pure, cold certainty playing across his face.

'I would be sitting right where I am now,' he replied in a monotone. 'This is what I do, and I see no reason to cease when I am clearly so incredibly good at it.'

In that instant, all my doubts and hesitancy at leaving the markets were dispelled in a flash; he had distilled the essence of his addiction perfectly. It was the same obsession I had been slave to for six long years, and the compulsion that has ensnared thousands of other traders and dealers.

What begins as the means to get rich quick or die trying soon metamorphoses in many to become the end in itself. Trading was all that Simon now saw himself put on this earth to do, and no sum of money was large enough to prevent him carrying out his task till his dying day. He was as hooked on his fix as the junkies in squats half a mile away on the Fulham Road: he hit his computerized

crack pipe for hours every day, but rather than be casti-
gated for his weakness by society, he was hoisted upon
their shoulders and declared a hero to legions of eager
young acolytes.

His life was the ultimate cautionary tale for those
seeking to avoid the habit-forming trap of the markets;
yet, even as the realization dawned upon me, I still gazed
upon his visage with the adoration of a pilgrim glimps-
ing a saint. I'd taken the boy out of the City, but I'd never
quite get the City out of the boy.

'You'd better pull up a chair,' says Simon, as he prepares
to deliver his keynote speech to a one-man audience.
What follows is a stream of consciousness, tearing into
the man he feels is the real culprit of the hour, the real
instigator of the credit crisis: one Gordon Brown, British
Prime Minister and former Chancellor of the Exchequer.
In Simon's eyes, Brown is responsible for the 'greatest
peacetime deception ever', a weighty bat to swing in the
PM's direction.

This is a topic Cawkwell has been thinking about
long and hard for years: that the bubble has finally burst
reassures him that he was right all along. In May 2003 he
sounded a cautionary warning during a speech he was
delivering at an investment conference, in which he
described the penchant for freely granting credit as
'absolutely staggering'. He noted that much of the
money 'sloshing around' had been raised by remortgag-
ing properties – amounting to around £35 billion in
2003 alone, by his reckoning. 'This, of course, is total
insanity,' he remarked at the time, 'because this debt will
have to be repaid out of what will inevitably, in the end,
prove to be a declining asset. I don't know where it will
end, but it will happen. It has to happen: that's the nature

of gravity.' Now that the chickens have come home to roost, he emphatically points the finger at those in the highest corridors of power.

'It's a fact that throughout human history there have been cycles in the granting and taking of credit,' he says. 'The central lie that Brown started with was "an end to boom and bust". His view was that by his astute management of the economy there would be no more busts. He anaesthetized the British, because if he'd warned people that there would be a bust, people would have been much more cautious. He wanted them to keep being more reckless so he could tax them on the transient profits earned, and also he likes being re-elected – he couldn't have become Prime Minister if the British didn't think he was a good chap, and they knew he'd be a good chap if there weren't any busts. That was the deception.

'The moral justification of the deception is simple: by boiling up the economy he produces a lot of taxable activity, and with the taxes raised he can attend to his various social programmes. That's how he would justify it: he lied in the better interests of this country. Well, I don't agree,' says Cawkwell matter-of-factly, leaning back in his chair. 'It is bound to lead to trouble. After all, he must have known he was lucky getting away with the reflation of America after the collapse of Long Term Capital Management in 1998. And then he had a stroke of luck, which was the arrival of the internet and the housing boom, which caused people to go on borrowing, and finally he had the commodity boom. By then there were no possible other booms around, so the thing burst. Which it had to eventually; it becomes an intolerable pressure upon people, these collective obligations to repay. For every debit there's a credit.

'So the economy started to implode. It started here with Northern Rock – it was the first crack in the dam, so to speak. Although long before then most reasonable people thought it odd that pension funds were willing to put up cash into private equity deals. People were amazed by the extent to which credit was granted. Brown blames the bust upon sub-prime breaking, but it's an absolute nonsense. The truth is that any reasonable Chancellor of the Exchequer would have seen that things were not right and done something about it.

'There was a time when the Governor of the Bank of England would judge that there was too much credit being taken in the economy. But in a great show of modesty, Brown said to the British people, "I will take away the control of interest rates from the Chancellor and leave it with the Bank of England." It was a fake bit of modesty – it's not possible for the Chancellor of the day to distance himself from interest rate policy. The idea was to persuade the people that Brown was a humble fellow deferring to the judgement of the City.

'At the same time as this was going on, regulation of banks was left with the FSA. People assume that means everything is regulated, but it depends on what you mean by regulation of a bank. The FSA reviewed the conduct of banks as regards the proper running of a bank. So the idea was that amounts shown as recoverable on the bank's books could reasonably be expected to be recovered. Well that's fine. And, of course, the public – with the delightful silliness that makes up the public – said, well, that's inflation sorted, that's the banks sorted. But what happened was that, by default, the review of aggregate credit – as I say, the granting of credit and the taking of credit – went over to the Treasury, and, of course, that's exactly what Brown wanted, as it meant that no one would blow the whistle. No one had any statutory or mandated duty to say anything, with the result that nobody did say anything. And then Brown knew perfectly well that there were heroic rises of general indebtedness in the British economy, so as a result the borrowing went on and got worse and worse. This was a deliberate and sustained exercise in deception.

'Even if you adjust for inflation, the [borrowing] figures are enormous in terms of, say, percentage of earnings or percentage of gross domestic product, and as a result people are going to be rather disappointed whilst all this is being corrected. Of course, because Brown anaesthetized people not to worry about debt, they gaily spent, he taxed them, and spent the money on various loony [public sector] non-jobs. If you open the *Guardian* every day of the week – and I don't – you'll see tons of non-jobs there like "inequalities imposition adviser", or something like that. And it's a nice idea in a sense, but, of course, it's fantastically wasteful of taxpayers' money and it can't be sustained.'

At this point we are interrupted by the first of a barrage of phone calls, the post-lunch wave of brokers, bookies and fellow bettors calling to either seek Cawkwell's counsel or dispense their own words of wisdom. He is in his element. As the *Guardian* put it in 2002, 'he is a big man with an even bigger reputation. His words can inflict mortal damage on a company, his share dealings make or lose him millions in moments. He is a puncturer of pomposity, an ingénu prepared to tell the emperor that he is butt naked. At least, that is how his fans view him ... At 20 stone, and with a laugh that doubles as a fog horn, he is the City's most famous contrarian.'

Cawkwell's incarnation as Evil Knievel began in 1990,

when he used the nom de plume on a devastating research note he published about Maxwell Communication Corporation. In the study, he demonstrated that, without some nifty accounting, the company would have made a loss of £200 million. The Evil Knievel name stuck, with journalists playing their part in mythologizing the character and cementing his reputation in market folklore. David Buik of Cantor Index described him as 'incredibly bright, he just goes down to the fundamentals. He understands balance sheets and he's as tough as teak.'

That description fits the character I first came across in 2002, when I was handed his account to look after. Cawkwell has lost none of his zeal for trading and amassing wealth at the expense on those on the losing side of his deals. Whilst he has allowed me to spend the afternoon plaguing him with questions, he still spends the majority of our time together with his eyes fixed on the bank of screens atop his desk.

After he's finished his scathing attack on Brown and dealt sharply with the next caller, he fills me in on his formative years in the market.

'I've always been a gambler, and the stock market is all about gambling, so it's natural enough [that I was drawn towards it]. But that wasn't how I started off,' he recalls. 'I was interested in politics at school. One of the ideas that was raised was whether through political change the economy could be made more efficient and thus people would enjoy the benefits. Of course, once you start [thinking about] that, you wonder about the performance of companies on an individual basis rather than on a global basis – at least that was how it seemed to me. So it was only natural to form an opinion about shares quoted on the London Stock Exchange.'

He began placing bets at sixteen – ten shillings on a horse. His debut trade was effected around six years later.

'I think the first share I ever bought was probably Lonrho. I can't remember how long I held it; I lost money on it, that's for sure,' he laughs. He didn't study the company report and accounts, but 'I thought it was an impressive idea that money could – and would – be made in Africa. Of course, I didn't realize at all that Tiny Rowland spent his entire time bribing African presidents.'

It's a different story today. Since he became a full-time investor/trader, managing his family's investments (he is married with two daughters), he's taken the business as seriously as any other fund manager.

'I wake up at about 4.30 a.m., and my newspapers arrive here very early. I check my [trading] positions and put on Bloomberg. Then I trade the market, if there is something to be done.'

In his second book, *Evil's Good*, he conceded that this compulsive behaviour indicated a form of addiction: 'My addiction to gambling and the market rather pathetically does not let me lift my eyes from the screen.' A few pages later, he mused on what he would do to enjoy himself 'if I were a free man'. For someone who has made millions of pounds per annum to describe themselves as anything but free is extraordinary. As well as being addicted to the gambling element of the market, he sees trading and investing as an intellectual challenge in much the same vein as crossword puzzles: '[There's always another] problem, and you've got to think about it,' he says. But he is quick to draw a distinction about pastimes involving a monetary prize. 'If you don't have the money [involved], it's like playing poker without money, and you can't do that. You've got to go out on a limb, you see, and bet.'

He won't stop trading 'until I go gaga', he assures me. There is no monetary watermark that, once breached, would make him hang up his boots, since it is not simply money that drives him: 'I enjoy it. The matter interests me.' It's a solitary existence – just him and his screens, as opposed to the life of a prop trader in a room surrounded by dozens of other dealers – but Cawkwell is sanguine. 'I can usually be seduced to go out to lunch – if it's a nice lunch [on offer].'

His years in the market, during which he has had his share of stunning victories and equally heavy losses, have taught him how to approach the volatility of equities and indices.

'It's very important not to overreact. Often the best advice is not to react at all. Stop losses [setting a level for the share price, which, once breached, compels the investor to close his position to avoid further losses on the trade] are a complete waste of time, since on a fast-moving stock, in particular a smaller company, it goes straight through the stop loss and you can't get it.'

However self-discipline is vital to success since – in gambling as much as anywhere else – pride comes before a fall.

'I'm prepared to take a loss,' he says, maintaining that he feels no sense of shame should he be forced to close out a losing position. 'The only time when I feel a sense of injured pride is when a margin clerk insists upon cutting a position [forcibly closing the trade on the basis that insufficient funds are held in the account] because I can't put up the cash, and I just say that means trading without economic reason. And he says put up the cash, and I say for God's sake just let everything run, and they won't – and that irritates me intensely.'

The list of his winning trades is endless – this year alone, he expects to make around £3 million in profit, including the £250,000 he made in less than an hour during one trading session in October. He also famously made a million pounds just from shorting Northern Rock the previous year, when the government was eventually forced to privatize the ailing lender.

'I work on the assumption that I'm intellectually superior to ninety-nine people out of a hundred,' he explained to the press in late 2008. 'And I'd give the other man a good run for his money.'

'I do like to beat the market,' he tells me. 'And it's not easy to beat the market. People say it's easy, and they're wrong. I think it is very important to bear in mind how participants of the market think. If you don't do that, you don't know why the market's doing what it's doing.'

At this point, he gets sidetracked by Man Group, a hedge-fund goliath whose shares have been battered over the course of the day, losing over 30 per cent in value.

'I'm not short of them,' he tells me; his interest in the stock simply academic for the time being. 'I lost a lot of money on Man on the way up. I thought I would leave them alone, and now you can see the thing has finally broken, and that's it. They went over 300p this morning, and I thought, well, I really ought to sell them; then I said no, no, not now, wait until they bounce and then have a look at it – and you can see what's happened; it's down another 40p.'

He and his market contacts keep up a steady stream of conversation, exchanging thoughts about the state of the FTSE and where it's likely to go next.

'I told one man I'd be selling the index when it was down 100 [points]. Now it's down 250 – I think that's quite good.'

How did he know the market would continue falling?

'Oh, because I knew that they would misinterpret the interest rate cut [a mammoth 1.5 per cent cut announced earlier in the day]. You see, the market was down 200 [before the news], and actually I'd have stayed short there, but my friend said I'm going to cover the short and wait until the announcement. So, as soon as the announcement was out of the way, the index went to at one stage down just sixty or seventy, and I thought this is a terrific sell, because the reason for the low interest rates is the catastrophic decline of economic activity. And, as a result of that, I thought it's got to be sold, because when people start looking at the effect on earnings, I mean, golly ... I knew that, with a reduction of 1.5 percentage points, the market would initially receive that as bullish, because that's the way people are – and they did: the market shot up on the announcement. But I knew that when people had thought about it [some more], then the market would go down.'

As it did – like a lead balloon. Always with an eye on the next trading opportunity, Simon is already considering what to do once the dust has settled on the day's move in the FTSE.

'I'd want to have a look overnight and see how it goes, but I'd probably be a buyer on the opening tomorrow I should think – the market always overreacts.'

The market is most certainly not a glorified casino, he states forcefully.

'Casinos have in a sense random results, save that in the long term all the results are in the favour of the house.'

Despite blurring the lines when it comes to his own dealings, he clearly demarcates between trading the markets and backing horses, for example.

'Well [the market] is a gamble in the sense that the results are uncertain, but in the long run, astute investment is not gambling – it's like farming. [Whereas] betting on the horses is simply gambling – some you win, some you lose.'

Between more phone calls we discuss the way others might view his lifestyle and trading habits.

'I am arguably the most indifferent-to-public-opinion person in the land,' he replies, in languid, well-spoken tones. 'I simply don't care what anybody thinks, unless they disagree with me or agree with me. If they disagree they're wrong, if they agree with me they are inspired – by me,' he smiles. If some find it unpalatable to stake five-figure sums on horse races, he is unconcerned. 'Well, they're welcome to go on doing whatever they do, and I'll get on with whatever I like doing.'

As the market drifts towards the closing bell, he turns his attention to the night's European football action. Spotting a discrepancy between betting firms' odds for the Aston Villa/Slavia Prague match, he does some swift mental arithmetic and pounces. He's had his account closed at several bookmakers over the years, after taking too much money from them via his winning bets. In this instance, he is only allowed to place a £2,000 bet, rather than the £5,000 stake he'd hoped to put down.

I remind him of a story involving him, myself and my then-girlfriend, which occurred when I first moved to Israel. Not having severed the umbilical cord that bound me to the market, I kept an eye on both the betting and trading worlds. One day Bnei Sakhnin – an Israeli team – were due to make their UEFA Cup debut, playing away at Newcastle United in the first leg. Newcastle were 1/6 to win, a price prohibitively long for small-size punters, but one which I thought might interest Simon – so I called him from a beachside bar in Tel Aviv. I pointed out that he might fancy putting £60,000 on Newcastle to win £10,000 back. It looked like a dead cert, given who was playing and where. He politely declined, but told me if I was so certain about the bet, he would give me those odds, and I could stake £60,000 with him.

My girlfriend's eyes lit up, and she told me I'd be a fool not to back my judgement, urging me to take him up on his offer and make a quick ten grand. 'Don't be ridiculous', I replied, the size of the bet far larger than anything I'd ever staked on a football match. She went ballistic, sucked in by the prospect of a five-figure windfall, and detached from the reality of what would happen if I lost. When Newcastle duly won 2-0 she was even more furious – and tells me to this day that I should have followed my heart, despite the stratospheric sum I'd have been risking.

Discussing the story today, Simon agrees with my cautious stance.

'I think once you start betting on that basis, then you have crossed the Rubicon. People who do that get carried off to prison.'

'Will you now watch the Villa game?' I ask, as he continues to scout out the betting sites in search of anomalous prices.

'I might have a look at it, yes,' he replies. 'It won't change the result, I hasten to add.'

His attention swings back to the stock market once more, as he casts a derisive eye over a property company he is convinced is due to collapse into administration.

'It's a residential property investor, and it's bust. Just look at the figures they published, and you think, "Abandon hope all ye who enter here." I'm short of a couple of hundred thousand. I've done it from about £2.25, or was it £2.15? I'm just sitting there to wait until it's the end of the company.'

He moves on, bringing up the order book on another stock of which he's been perennially short.

'[This company] caused me grief about four years ago, so I said, right, I'll cause you grief, and it was all very childish. I see it's down again today – I've got to decide when to buy these things back. I sold them originally at 50p, sold them up again at £1, and now they are 10p to buy. I just think it's a badly run company, and so events have proved.'

And, with that final flourish, our session is over. Cawkwell swivels round to give the screens his undivided attention once more.

8. Falling into the Abyss

I've been clean of drugs for less time than I've been clean of trading, but there's no doubt which monkey's been harder to get off my back. Put a line of coke in front of me, and it'll conjure up memories of sleepless, tremor-filled nights. Put a dealing ticket and a SETS screen in front of me, and I'll be fired-up and ready to immerse myself in the thrill of the chase, in the overpowering rush of going live again in the market melee.

Trading brought me back to my senses after even the heaviest of nights. In *The Grass Arena*, John Healy's seminal autobiographical account of his descent into alcoholism and near-death in the streets and parks of inner London, his description of his first drink of the day beautifully mirrors the way I felt every morning as my first trade was placed: 'I needed a cure and found a bottle on Paddy's side of the bed. Put it to my lips. Felt the wine trickle down my throat into my stomach, feeding my veins, bringing back the confidence with which to start a new day.'

To a true addict, the quality of the product consumed makes no difference. A bottle of Château Lafite might be the ideal choice of the discerning drunk, but the minute the wine cellar's dry a cheap bottle of vodka will suffice, if the need to sink into wasted oblivion is strong enough. So it is with cocaine – whilst I never again found coke as smooth and powerful as the eighth I scored in a Havana backstreet one winter, I'd go as low as racking up lines of badly cut speed if my London charlie dealer's cupboard was bare.

So it is with trading. Sitting in my Jerusalem flat in October 2008, feeling the urge to be a part of the credit crisis in my own small way, I sling half a grand into my years-dormant online betting account and dive head-first into punting around on utterly banal FTSE-related bets. There is a market in predicting whether the level of the overall index would be higher or lower than it was twenty minutes earlier. That's about as close to market roulette as it gets, I think, until I notice Ladbrokes is making an even more hyperactive offer, allowing punters to bet on the movements over five-minute intervals.

My initial reaction is of elitist sneering at this type of betting that exists for those outside City circles; after all, these bets can't even affect the underlying market, since they are just matched off against contrary wagers from other punters (rather than with a spread-betting firm trading on the FTSE itself). However, once I overcome my scorn, I realize this is the best I am going to get if I can't be bothered to set up a proper spread-betting account. I swallow my pride and enter the fray.

Six hours later and I'm frozen in place, chain-smoking, CNBC blaring market updates from my wall-mounted plasma TV as I hunch over my laptop, my body contorted in flawless imitation of the pose I used to strike on a daily basis. Lists of hastily scribbled FTSE data sit on the table, marked by brown rings from half-finished mugs of cof-fee. I swivel my eyes on an endless, high-speed loop, from CNBC to the betting screen to the live FTSE graph and back, absorbing the numbers, words and oscillating lines with an automatic, involuntary instinct.

The amounts I have at stake are so paltry as to make it

utterly absurd to spend so much time on the activity. A fiver here, a tenner there, and the occasional £20 punt – a far cry from the six- and seven-figure trades I monitored for clients in my former life. But that's the proof that the Lafite/vodka analogy fits the situation in which I find myself. Instead of caring about whether I'm staking fifty grand or £50, it's all about the underlying lust to trade, to feel connected to a bigger picture. Despite my shredded nerves, I feel truly happy when my bets are running: a superficial and short-term happiness, maybe, but that doesn't matter in the moment. I'm instantly alert.

I was assailed with similar sensations upon walking back into a dealing room for the first time since emigrating to Israel. As I gazed adoringly at the flashing lights and scrolling news bars on the banks of Reuters and Bloomberg screens, the hairs on the back of my neck stood on end. Even though I had long convinced myself of the self-destructive nature of trading, the ultimate futility of endlessly pursuing wealth and never being satisfied however well I'd done, the doubts were relegated. Memories of my best trades bubbled to the fore, my heart conning my brain into believing that it had been a pain-free six-year sojourn in the Square Mile amusement arcade. I was like the gambler who only tells his friends about his big wins and never mentions the losses he's suffered in equal measure.

If I felt like this, having spent not much more than half a decade in the City – and at the lower, softer end of the scale at that – what of those for whom trading has spanned a far longer period and who gamble at higher-stakes tables? The results speak volumes about the true, corrosive side-effects of City life and read as a Belloc-style cautionary tale to anyone thinking that all is sweetness and light inside the gilt-edged ghetto of the Square Mile.

Jonny White's description of 'a pure driven trader' requiring 'balls of steel and a stinking horrible personality', as well as being 'a nasty person, a risk taker and a gambler', suggests a flawed value system. Yet, given the job description of the average trader, it's not hard to see why such characteristics are sought after by employers – which makes one wonder how it is that even more traders haven't fallen by the wayside, trampled beneath the stampede towards ever more, and ever faster-accumulated, wealth by the banking behemoths.

Plenty of those working in the City do feel used and abused by their employers. The central tenet upon which they all seem to agree is that trading is a habit-forming activity, a practice wholly conducive to addiction. It centres on instant gratification and cravings for a stronger high. Even once traders call time on their careers, they are still not free, as Paul O'Connor found out. He believes that working in the markets can rewire your mental systems.

'I think if you work in a certain environment and temptations get put in your way, it can push you towards it.'

Whilst he doesn't believe he has an addictive genetic make-up – 'I didn't just punt, there was always some thinking behind it' – he wasn't as immune as he first thought to the lure of making money the fast way.

'I began PA [personal account] trading because it just seemed to be an easy way to money,' he recalls. 'We were the insiders, we were the ones that had the information, and we were giving all these ideas to our clients. So why not take advantage of that and join in and make money? They do have strict controls at investment banks – you have to get compliance approval before you trade, and you have to hold an investment for thirty days – but there are ways round it. Like using a friend's account, or trading certain specific products. This is happening a lot at the moment. If you trade f/x or spread-bet, or trade indices, you don't have to get compliance approval, and you don't have to have the thirty-day holding rule. One of my ex-colleagues used to do a lot of this index trading, and he was half a million pounds in profit. But the markets have been so volatile he lost a million pounds [in 2008]. This is a guy who's earning a couple of hundred grand a year, and he lost a million.'

As for O'Connor's own trading, he makes no attempt to cover up the pain it caused him when things began to go wrong.

'It felt like shit, basically. It consumed me, last year when I lost money. I had two very bad experiences: one was on a Bangladeshi coal plant, and one was on Northern Rock. You try to convince yourself you are right and that it will turn in your favour. I invested in a coal plant, and then there was an environmental movement against it – a riot when somebody was killed. The Bangladeshi government cancelled the contract of the coal company, and the share price collapsed, and I found myself fifty grand down. I convinced myself that the contract would be reinstated because the Bangladeshi government had no other alternative – because coal was their only way of becoming energy sufficient, and the Marxists would be defeated – so I poured more money into my position. I threw good money after bad. It's very hard to accept that you were wrong, that you've had a loss. It's all-consuming: I wasn't sleeping, I started developing pains in my body, a neck ache that wouldn't go away, every time I thought about it I felt sick . . .

'I remember with Northern Rock my partner and I had a really nice holiday planned in France. I ruined my holiday, fucking ruined it, because every time I woke up I thought I've just fucking lost fifty grand. What made it worse – and I think you can tell now that I'm still getting rankled – is that I worked fucking hard for that money, I was taxed 40 per cent on that money, and it's just gone, pissed up the wall.'

He did not, however, throw more cash at Northern Rock, recognizing that 'doubling up' is a favoured tactic of more extreme gamblers. We discuss whether, as some psychologists maintain, gamblers actually take a perverse pleasure from losing, sometimes enjoying the sensation even more than when they win.

Is there an element of sadness once the bet is closed, I ask, regardless of whether one has made or lost money? Does the thrill of the chase result in what some call a post-coital lull?

'I know what you mean,' he replies. 'It's the closure, and it is almost post-coital,' although he makes an important distinction: 'When you've made the money, you get that orgasmic, satiated feeling, but when you've closed the losing position, you just feel "Was it really worth it?" You've fulfilled the need, but it doesn't feel good.'

However, he still reminisces fondly on the upside of his dealing.

'I remember when I made money on my PA account, I booked a holiday to Barbados and thought the holiday was even better because it's free.'

To hear PA profits described as 'free' money is strange. The description seems to be buying into the concept that PA trading is not money properly earned, as though there is no downside to the bet being wagered. O'Connor speaks in the same self-deprecating tones when discussing the salary he took home.

'When I got paid a lot of money, I felt guilty. I thought, why am I being paid half a million pounds when I'm not doing that much? I was working twelve, thirteen, fourteen hours a day, but I didn't feel it was worth it. My biggest pay packet was 700 grand, and even now I don't think I deserved it. Because I didn't feel I was working that hard – I used to make my calls in the morning, do some deals, but I'd take two hours off and surf online . . . it was too much, too young.'

He expands on this theory as an explanation for the downfall of many a trader, as well as well-paid employees in other industries.

'The City gives young people too much money too quickly. In the same way they say it about celebrity, people who become too famous too young, it can fuck them up – like Robbie Williams, and footballers like Beckham and Rooney. I didn't get successful till later in life – I didn't start earning big money until my early thirties, and I'm glad.

'My brother became a derivatives trader, earning big money in his early twenties, and it fucked him up. We were looking to buy a house together one Saturday morning and we popped into a pub, and he burst into tears. It was the pressure of being a derivatives trader with his own book. He had a position which was going wrong, and the pressure of trying to earn money to keep his money where it was, to earn enough money in order to get paid more, got too much. His low point came when he was driving to work one day, age twenty-five, in a new Saab convertible, and thought, "I wish I could crash and go to hospital, so I wouldn't have to go to work." That was a direct result of being paid too much, too young, and he couldn't live up to the pressure of justifying that money.'

However, in Paul's view, the days of millionaire teen-aged traders are numbered.

'All this about twenty-one-year-olds earning a million pounds, that's utter bollocks – that doesn't happen any more. Maybe it still goes on in the hedge-fund world, but I think those days are kind of over.'

Over in the hedge funds, a jaded Rob Davis asserts that he has 'fallen out of love with trading a little bit. When my kid came along, I suddenly realized there was so much more to life.'

That realization was exacerbated by stress.

'Whatever money I earn, the City's given me major anxiety issues. It probably all started when I was a private client stockbroker and I'd lost a bit of money for some clients. I got movements in my muscles that I thought was motor neurone disease, but it's all nerves. I was see-ing someone about it at the Priory [a rehabilitation clinic]. Everyone thinks, "Rob works in the City, he drives around in a Lotus, he lives in a nice house in Notting Hill," but ultimately I just come home and I want to see my kid. That's when I'm happy.

'At the moment, there's a lot of extra stress; people are very nervous about putting their trades on. I'm long of half a million Tesco right now, and I can't stop looking at them. [Which is crazy, because] it's just half a million Tesco: I'm supposed to be running $200 million. I'm thinking about my positions at night. I was going to bed, this time last year, when I had a bad position in a UK small-cap company which I knew was a good company, and I was waking up shouting its name in the middle of the night.

'If I go and buy five million shares of Vodafone, it makes me anxious. That said, I'm in control of the situation, I know what my likely outcome will be. I know what my downside is, but my upside could be anything as well – that's where the buzz is. I've learned how to deal with the anxiety, I've sought a lot of help. I've learned how to deal with different situations, so if I'm buying a million shares of Marks and Spencer, I know what my ultimate downside is. You've got to learn to think about what's really important. So what if I lose 250 grand, I'm running a $200 million book. Just learn to know what's more important. You walk in the door and see your kid run up to you to give you a cuddle, and you think, fuck the M&S trade.'

The shock of the credit crisis and the ensuing volatility of the markets haven't helped Davis cope with the stress.

'That's an element of why I'm not putting on the big trades at the moment. I'm holding back because I'm scared. But my bosses say, "Don't be scared: it's not your money, you're not going to prison if you get it wrong." But it's just holding me back.'

Whilst there are some people he can approach with his problems, showing vulnerability is not always the best option in such a tough environment.

'You don't want to turn to some people and tell them, "I'm suffering from anxiety," because they'll say, "Well, you might as well get out of this job." But everyone suffers from it. Suddenly you get a mental block – and it's all about confidence in the City.'

While trading has clearly taken a heavy emotional and physical toll on Davis, he has nevertheless made a handsome living – and his superiors have banked tens of millions of pounds from their careers. I ask Davis why these guys still trade.

'If you're worth £100 million you treat it like a bit of a game, a bit of fun, whereas if I trade and don't make any money for a year that affects me.

'One of my bosses is an addict. He's not bothered if he buys a million shares of Rio Tinto and they go down a quid, because ultimately he's got so much money behind him. His type become more and more addicted, because they've made money so they can take the bigger risk. He traded on his sister's wedding day while the ceremony was going on, he traded from his suite at Sandy Lane on his wedding anniversary. A good friend of mine will be at our house for dinner, sitting there with the markets on his Blackberry – he cannot leave it. Always looking for the next money-making opportunity.

'I probably am an addict as well, because I'm desperate to know what the market's doing right now,' Davis continues. 'In a way, when the market's closed on a Saturday and Sunday it's a pleasure, because sometimes it's just too much . . .'

He may be an addict, but he's not a gambler, he says – adding weight to the thesis that trading itself is the addictive element of the job, rather than an innate love of gambling.

'I do love trading, because it's more calculated than gambling, and I'm good at it. I can't tell you whether Arsenal are going to come back from 1–0 down against Chelsea, but I can tell whether Tesco are going to go up. It's from years of looking at charts and getting a gut feel.'

Futures trader Damien Walsh speaks with cast-iron certainty about the addictive nature of his job.

'Discipline is 100 per cent vital in trading,' he states.

'And this is where addiction comes in, because addiction is the opposite of discipline in a sense. In these circumstances, the inability to rein yourself in and to have to constrict yourself in what you do is a lack of discipline, and it encourages an addiction. But the thing is that, since trading began, instead of curbing addiction, there have been ways to prevent the addiction proving too big a loss. So every fucking trader's got limits. On every trade they do, there's a limit. That is a direct admission that the trader cannot control themselves.

'Trading is so much stronger than alcohol in that respect: you're not legally obliged to say when you walk into the pub, "I'm only having two pints," and then they only give you two pints. But with traders, they do not take that risk. Maybe it's because there's a lot more at stake, but I think it's more because traders can't be trusted. People that are forced into working as hard as they can and putting their all into something, they're not going to be able to control themselves when it comes to giving up because they got it wrong.'

He remembers the first time he broke his own limit, a watershed moment.

'That's the worst thing, when you break a limit and then end up making money, because it tells you that maybe the discipline that they enforce on you isn't necessarily correct. But, you know, if you're not the kind of person that's going to try and break your limits once in a while, you're not the kind of person that's going to make serious money. Because the difference between someone that fucking floats along doing nothing, making fifty grand a year, and someone that makes 100, 200, 500 grand a year is in having the balls. You see the people that do well, and they've got enormous *cojones*.

'Trading is a natural addiction,' he continues. 'Everyone's addicted to making money. You have to make money to survive in the world. Trading is the way to make money quickest. I've seen them try to rein in big traders, and it's very hard because they know their potential even better than the people that they're making money for. I've seen people being dragged away from their computers. With drugs and alcohol, you have experiences which make them less addictive, but with trading there's no bad trip or side-effects that might make you stop. If you're losing money you're going to keep trading until they stop you.'

Walsh recalls a former colleague who was trading stocks.

'One day someone walked past his screen [and saw that] he was long on CAC [French index futures], short on DAX [German index futures] and long on Eurostoxx [futures on a basket of blue-chip Eurozone stocks]. It was the most insane position – he had already lost about ten grand – so he got kicked out. A year later someone got a call from him saying, "Can I borrow some money? I owe 200 grand on ten different credit cards. I've been spread-betting currencies." Some of these people spend their lives believing they have the potential to make big money, yet never do it.'

Walsh suffered similar symptoms to Davis.

'I used to wake up every hour and a half; I wanted to check prices all the time. It's very hard to try and absorb all this information during the trading day and still maintain some kind of life, so you become obsessive about it. You trade twelve hours a day, you sleep hopefully six. That means you've got six hours in which to shower, eat, travel and see your friends. I don't think anyone goes into trading that doesn't have an arrogance

and a competitiveness, although these things don't necessarily make a good trader. Neither does being smart
or having a degree in economics.'

Walsh had a natural affinity to the markets from the
off.

'It always suited my personality. I never had any patience,
and that's why I like the job. Because I'm really busy all
the time, except when it gets to dry periods when the
markets are too hard to trade. I've always been bad at sitting on my hands, so I smoke a lot of cigarettes and I go
for a walk. I pace around the outside of the office. I do a
couple of laps before I think about my trade. Because the
pressure leads to you second-guessing yourself, and that's
the worst thing you can do. There's so much psychology
involved with trading; it's all-encompassing. To succeed
you have to involve yourself entirely, and anything short of
that means there's no point your being there.

'It's not just a fucking punt on a hobby of yours, or a
love of a team. It's your life, it's your livelihood. It's your
family. It's everything. Because there is always the opportunity to make money, plenty of people just switch to a
new market when the [home] market shuts. Plenty of
people go home and play poker. During quiet times, in
the summer, you can go to a trading floor and watch
them playing two or three games of poker at a time. These
are people that have to face embracing risk all day, every
day. Every time they do anything, they are asking for risk;
if it's taken away from them they have withdrawals.

'Again, it is their choice to begin with. I'm not saying
it's an unfair life. They reap the rewards, and it's a sweet
life they get at the end of it if they get it right, but at the
same time it's tough. It's always going to be something
you want more of, because when you get it wrong you

want to get it right, and when you get it right you want
to do it again.'

I ask him why trading has managed to retain an air of
respectability about it, at least in the sense that it is still
not only entirely legal, but part of an industry viewed by
parents as a suitable career choice for their offspring.

'There are millions of acceptable forms of addiction,'
he replies. 'A glass of wine a day is an acceptable form of
addiction. Smoking is a semi-acceptable addiction. The
addiction to trading is seen as a slight downside, with the
money being a massive upside. I don't think anyone cares
about it being seriously damaging. I've seen people unable to give up. I've been unable to give it up. I've gone
over my limits. Before I can rack up a big debt, it goes
through ten people or so. That indicates that I am
addicted because they are permitting me a fix, and every
day I get a fix of how much I can trade.'

He concurs that this never leaves the bloodstream: 'If
you turned on CNBC now, I'd want to trade straight
away. If you gave me 100 grand now, I'd trade it instantly.'
And he recalls the intense level of anxiety before a major
market announcement.

'You will never be nervous about anything like I used
to be nervous of Non-Farm Payrolls [US economic data
revealing the level of unemployment in the nation]. Half
an hour before it came out I wouldn't be able to sit
down. My hands would be sweating. I wouldn't be able
to say anything. I knew it could go either way. It could
go all the way up and then all the way down and back
up again, or do twenty points and then reverse 100
points. Who fucking knows?'

He speaks with the anxiety of a goalkeeper awaiting
the penalty kick.

'People in regular jobs have to make a decision like this once a year. A fucking MP, governments, they don't make any decisions. This is exactly why trading is such a hard job, because that's what a trader does from day one. They are seriously hard decisions, they have massive consequences, and they have to be both learned from and ignored simultaneously. In no other job are you so responsible for your own destiny. In no other job are you so responsible for so much. And in no other job is so much invested into you.'

Since Walsh runs his own book, he feels as though he is trading for his own direct benefit on a daily basis without feeling the need to deal PA as well. Michael Parnes, on the other hand – as a broker rather than trader – was tempted to deal for himself on occasion.

'I was always told by my dad that the beauty of being a broker is that you don't need to take the risk yourself. That's not to say you're irresponsible with other people's money, but it's riskless being a broker – regardless of the client making or losing money you take a commission. So, why jeopardize that by taking risks yourself? I deal very rarely for myself, but I dealt in RBS recently, I made a bit of money, and I thought, wow, this is quite good fun, I could make a separate income. But it clouds your judgement. I then went in again and lost all of it and more, so I won't speculate again. I got burned.'

Reason eventually triumphed, since Parnes didn't succumb to an urge to chase his losses.

'Luckily I had the discipline and the sense to say, all right fine; I was always prepared to lose the whole holding. I wouldn't have invested otherwise. I was depressed [though].'

And if I was to show him the graph of RBS shares right now?

'No. Not even tempted, because of that pain that I felt. Some people haven't got that discipline; you see Nick Leeson and others who don't know when to cut it.'

While Walsh maintains that there is no bad-trip element to proprietary trading on a firm's book, nevertheless the experiences of both Paul O'Connor and Michael Parnes suggest that some financiers' commitment to their PA trading can be derailed in such a fashion. I am the same with casinos – having only visited two in my life, one in Warsaw, the other in Melbourne, and having lost money both times, I have no desire to set foot in one again. To avoid being sucked into the lifestyle and lure of easy money, some say it would be better to lose your first bet or trade so that you are put off it for life.

It's easier to take such evasive action when your working life isn't centred around trading or gambling; if you trade for a living, then the peer pressure and expectations of your superiors doesn't allow you to use the escape route. With no health warnings surrounding the City, there is even less of an incentive to view the activity as destructive. This, combined with the demand by firms and clients for ever-larger returns, means traders are swept away in the pursuit of instant gratification.

Once one's trading virginity is lost, the spiral into all-consuming addiction can be swift, a process I discuss with psychoanalyst Coline Covington.

'Addiction is something that is compulsive behaviour, where you can't stop,' she explains. 'There's a difference between an environment that is conducive to addictive behaviour, and a person who has an addictive personality.'

She believes in the latter concept: 'There are some people who do become addicted to alcohol, drugs or trading, who, if they didn't become addicted to that, would become addicted to something else. There is a certain element where it's genetically inherited, but there's also a strong link to very early issues of separation and attachment. If as a baby you didn't have a strong attachment with your mother, then you feel insecure. You then spend life looking for something else to hold on to, that you are in control of – or have the illusion that you're in control of. That's the core of an addictive disturbance.'

This characteristic is not restricted simply to activities deemed negative, such as drugs, gambling or alcohol; pursuits such as exercise or shopping can also become compulsive in the wrong hands.

'The reason it becomes destructive is because there is a power trip involved,' Covington says. 'That makes you say, "Fuck reality, I don't need to follow the rules, I don't need to face the sadness or the loss."'

In her experience, most addicts have had such experiences in their formative years.

I put it to her that – despite how my own experiences might appear to an observer – I have always been able to turn my seemingly compulsive behaviour on and off like a tap. When I was sitting in Jerusalem with nothing to do, I dived into betting on the markets with zeal, but the minute I was busy again the thought of gambling didn't cross my mind. Similarly, whilst I spent three years heavily into cocaine, as soon as I carved out a more intellectually and physically challenging life for myself – beginning in the Israeli army and later in writing for a living – the urge to take coke dissipated.

She tells me that, from the little she knows of me after our hour-long conversation, it sounds like I don't have an addictive personality – compared to many of the traders

I've interviewed, especially given the language they employed to describe their predicaments.

'I think that, when people use that kind of language, unless they're using it glibly, they are being honest. The question is, what is it that's trapping them? It's usually something inside themselves that makes them feel trapped, where they can't fight it, where they feel compelled to earn a lot of money or go along with this culture where there's no space for being needy or weak or having feelings. But, of course, if you're like that anyway, if you feel ashamed of your needs, if you feel ashamed of your feelings, then that's the kind of culture you're attracted to. It's like being a gladiator.'

The fired-up, gladiatorial aspect of trading is something studied in detail of late, as experts seek explanations for the post-credit-crunch collapse in traders' confidence. A study published in the *Proceedings of the National Academy of Sciences* found a strong link between traders' hormone levels and the way the markets gyrate. As reported in *The New York Times*, the researchers discovered that those traders with higher testosterone levels in the morning were more likely to make money during the day's trading. This leads into 'winner effect', where men get a testosterone boost when they win, meaning that they have an advantage going into the next battle.

'You can get a positive feedback loop between winning, testosterone [production], greater confidence and risk taking,' according to John Coates, one of the authors of the study. However, he believes that there is a point when traders' levels of testosterone are too high and they begin to take irrational risks with their dealing, which can lead to the markets collapsing. Cortisol – a stress hormone – is then put into play. It is produced in larger quantities during volatile periods in the market and gives rise to clouded judgement.

'You tend to see danger everywhere rather than opportunity,' Dr Coates says, helping to explain why traders like Rob Davis find themselves paralysed and unable to trade in the current climate. 'Fear takes over, so they are no longer thinking rationally, or doing the things that they should be doing to make money.'

Dr Coates believes that 'testosterone doesn't create bubbles, but it exaggerates them. It's possible that bubbles are a male phenomenon,' he continues, adding weight to some City observers' theory that adding more women into what is a heavily male-dominated environment could help stabilize dealing rooms and the market as a whole.

Covington agrees: 'It's a kind of adrenaline, you get a rush from it, and so physically you can get addicted to that. That's almost like a physical addiction; there's an element of it where you're producing a drug for yourself.'

We move on to discuss the hypothesis that some gamblers love to lose.

'There's something self-destructive, and you can get pleasure out of hurting yourself,' she says. 'I would certainly go along with the fact that, if you're doing something destructive, there is an element of pleasure in hurting yourself – in destroying yourself even – because it gives you a sense, paradoxically, of power.'

I tell her about my time boxing three times a week at a Jerusalem club, a pastime that held me utterly spellbound, despite the likelihood that I would suffer some form of injury every time I stepped into the ring.

'What you're talking about, in a way, is the pleasure and excitement of getting beaten up, and that's the masochism.'

It's the same with drugs, I muse. Even though I was aware that, for every night I spent racking up lines, I would go through torment during the comedown, it didn't stop me.

She replies, 'What's going on in that pleasure is that there's an attack inside of you against this vulnerable part of yourself. It's like beating yourself up, or allowing yourself to be beaten up. There's a little part of you that's thinking, I'll get out of this. In the end you believe you'll win because you don't have to pay attention to reality, and even if you're killing yourself, you've won. It is quite perverse.'

I ask her why so little attention is paid by either the FSA or firms to the mental state of those trading billions of pounds on a daily basis. Why is there a 'know your client' code but not a 'know your trader' equivalent? She tells me that several City firms and banks do take just such an interest in their staff, but agrees that it's not widespread.

'Maybe it's up to the government to stipulate that [firms] have to do that. It's an interesting question, how do you provide an MOT for traders, because other professions have that: accountants go through regular reviews [with official bodies], lawyers do, I do in my own practice.'

In one of his own books, Simon Cawkwell quotes from the *Encyclopaedia Britannica*, where it states that 'gamblers frequently experienced, or think that they experienced, absolute authority in childhood'.

'That rings bells,' says Covington, 'because gamblers are a bit different from alcoholics. There is a certain omnipotence about gamblers, and an arrogance. It's the swagger, and gamblers probably do have the idea that they can do what they want, come out on top, manipulate people – that they can pull rabbits out of the hat.'

However, this sense of self-belief can be the final nail in some gamblers' coffins. A trader who is used to making

1 or 2 per cent profits or losses on a steady basis can – once he suffers a sustained set of losing trades – rack up enormous losses trying to scramble out of the abyss.

'When you begin to lose, and then start losing even more, you still think you can turn things around by pulling that rabbit out of a hat,' says Covington. 'So instead of pulling a rabbit out, you need to pull out an elephant. Stopping is the problem, because you keep thinking, I can win this round – and then you lose, and the incentive to win is even greater. You start putting bigger amounts down – it's terribly dangerous.'

This is where a trader's adherence to the market advice to never throw good money after bad often gets suspended, their common sense replaced by an all-consuming conviction that they will eventually dig themselves out of trouble.

The faceless, man-versus-machine element of trading also adds fuel to the addictive fire, Covington says.

'You don't have this one-to-one interaction with people, because you can do it on your own – in a sense it's the sort of masturbatory aspect.'

The quick gratification of trading provides yet another layer to its habit-forming potential, in the same way that a line of coke or shot of vodka is used to fast-track a person towards the state of mind that would take them longer to achieve without artificial assistance.

'You get the same release, but what you don't get is the same satisfaction, and that's part of the reason why it's addictive,' she explains. 'If you cut corners all the time, you're left feeling empty inside. You haven't actually worked for anything, you haven't allowed yourself to be given anything either; you're caught on this treadmill of wanting to have more and more. Even though the addict might realize that if they do more of their drug of choice they will still feel hungry for more at the end, they keep on with the action, since it is so [overwhelmingly] addictive.'

Why doesn't a trader who's already banked £50 million simply retire and walk away from the market?

'Because it's not enough, and it can never be enough, because there's no relationship involved,' she replies. 'It's not satisfying after a while.'

A study of New York brokers in 2000 confirms this line of reasoning, reported Oliver James in the *Guardian*. Two-thirds of the subjects were depressed, with similar numbers suffering from sleeplessness or anxiety. The more money they earned, the more prevalent these problems became.

I suggest to Covington that this is related to status anxiety: no matter how much each broker or trader makes, there is always someone else in the City richer than them. The study suggests that those who go into finance believing cash will bring them contentment find that the opposite is true – that with the money comes the misery, as well as a shift away from their original motivations.

'I think people go into the City primarily to make money,' she observes, 'and to make life easier for themselves. But inevitably there will be people where money simply becomes the means and the ends to everything.'

Is money a mind-altering substance helping those who crave it escape from their other problems?

'It can be,' replies Covington, 'but it needn't be. There are plenty of people who have made quite a lot of money and do stop, who say, "I've made enough, this is what I want to do," and who go into charity work or change their lives in other ways. However, for others it may be a replacement for relationships which provide satisfaction. One of the motivations to make huge amounts of money is that other people will envy you – and so you don't have to be aware of your envious feelings towards others.'

Given all of the above, it's not unreasonable to see the City as a wholly corrosive environment. It foments greed, envy and addiction, and – by encouraging people to let out these feelings – it creates a monster. Although governments and health experts generally ban or restrict activities deemed harmful to individuals or those around them, there is no chance that trading, for example, or any of the other highly corrosive facets of the City will ever be outlawed for the public good. Instead entrants into the markets will continue to be reprogrammed and told to bring to the fore all of their negative traits, the kind of traits that those in other arenas might try and damp down.

'You do wonder how to inject some kind of different values in the City,' says Covington. 'But I don't think it is possible, because it's the nature of the beast. The question's more how you contain it and control it, how you regulate it.'

Finally we discuss why those who profess to be so depressed carry on slaving away in the bowels of the City. Those who say they feel trapped, that they hate their lives – why don't they just walk away?

'You have to be careful there,' replies Coline. 'When they say they're trapped, they're probably right. It's not the wife that's trapping them, for example, but something within themselves. That's a very masochistic mentality: "I'm a victim, I can't help it." That's the message that they're conveying to you, and it's baloney – but it indicates they feel like a victim and are being quite self-destructive at the same time. They say other people make them do this, make them suffer.'

Looking back at my own time in the City, I never felt trapped in the sense that Covington describes, but that had more to do with how young I was – and how few external responsibilities I had – than any great mental acrobatics. There is even a sense of *recherche du temps perdu* when I recall how attractive I found certain aspects of my City sojourn. But for those whose time in the Square Mile is anything but comfortable, the descent into their own private hells is swift, and often irreversible.

9. A Roll-call of Rogues

In recent years there have been high-profile cases involving market professionals who, despite auspicious beginnings, have come crashing down to earth in devastating fashion. Their sorry stories have engulfed them and their families, and often the firms for whom they worked and the shareholders whose money was caught up in the crises. The press has, unsurprisingly, had a field day covering the events, and the public has lapped up the tales with a mixture of schadenfreude and sympathy. Whatever the response, the underlying stories bear witness to the dangers posed by giving such power to, and putting such pressure on, individual traders and bankers in the ongoing drive for higher profits and instant returns.

In September 2007, Darren Liddle – a trader who had achieved Credit Suisse's best-ever first-year trading figures – threw himself from the nineteenth floor of the Park Lane Hilton. He had spent the night taking cocaine and drinking from the hotel minibar before slashing his wrists and jumping to his death, with his girlfriend and police looking on. According to the *Daily Telegraph*, the coroner in charge of the inquest blamed the pressure of working on the trading floor for his descent into drug abuse, a state of affairs which had led to him being sectioned twice in the year that he died.

Drugs played a major part in the downfall of another high-flying broker, who in early 2008 was given a suspended sentence for dealing in cocaine. Stephen Crump, who once earned £250,000 a year, was arrested by undercover police during a Met operation which uncovered a number of cocaine dealers selling drugs to City workers. Katharine Barney in the *Evening Standard* reported that three other dealers, who sold between £20,000 and £30,000 worth of the drug a week to office workers in their lunch breaks, were also caught during the sting and subsequently jailed.

Crump said he was offered cocaine almost immediately after starting work in the City aged seventeen, and by the peak of his addiction was spending £400 a day on cocaine, as well as drinking two bottles of wine, ten pints of lager and a bottle of vodka.

'The pressures were immense and everyone was doing it. You would hear sniffing in the toilets,' he said. 'We would start work at 6.30 a.m., take our first line at 11.30 a.m., then be entertaining until 2 a.m. I was very young and impressionable and suddenly I was earning all this money. I then became involved in a co-dependent relationship and would get home and carry on doing cocaine and drinking, then have a shower and go back to work. I was working in Singapore, Tokyo and Hong Kong, flying first-class on holiday to Barbados and buying £2,000 Gucci suits. Now everything is gone. But I've been clean for eighteen months and am pressing on, turning my life around and fighting to see my kids.'

A feature by Rob Sharp in the *Independent* describes the extent to which another trader lost control after turning to drink and drugs to cope with the stress of the City. In his article, Sharp describes a man named Dan Butcher going through a personal hell in which he'd sit in his car snorting coke for up to six hours at a time, somehow keeping his addiction a secret from everyone close to him, despite spending thousands of pounds a day on drugs. Butcher described himself as having been a shy kid who never fitted in as a trainee stockbroker.

'As well as working hard in a stressful environment, you were expected to go out with people in the office in the evenings and be part of a crowd,' he told Sharp. 'It was the early 1990s, and in those days it was all about hanging around in flashy nightclubs and ordering champagne.'

It wasn't long before the champagne he was drinking in order to keep up with his peers became cocaine that he had to snort to 'keep up'.

'That was the biggest mistake I ever made,' he told Sharp. 'I started using the drug on what I would describe as "special occasions", but along the way I started using it when I had a bad day at work. It made me forget about things.'

After ten years in the City Butcher felt that 'I could not function without it. By the late stages of that year, my day consisted of waking up and then having coke on my way to work. I had become so paranoid that by ten or eleven in the morning I could not bear to meet anyone else in the office. I would make any excuse not to run into people. I'd say I was playing golf, or in a meeting. But in reality I would be in my car doing coke.'

His addiction led to his admittance to the Priory for rehab, and then to his setting up The Recovery Network. Its aim is to help other addicts, no matter the drug of their choice.

Whilst some trading-room deviants detach themselves from reality by racking up lines of coke to get by, others rack up stratospheric losses on their firm's accounts in the vein of Nick Leeson, one of the original rogue traders. He spectacularly brought Barings Bank to its knees via his highly unauthorized, and highly unprofitable, trading; the losses eventually were set at over £800 million, and forced Barings to the wall.

More recently, two huge scandals rocked the French banking system, with over €5 billion worth of losses amassed between the trading desks of two well-established banks. In October 2008, French mutual bank Caisse d'Epargne announced a €751 million loss as a result of what it cryptically called a 'trading incident', after a small team of traders made a disastrous bet on the market.

Earlier in the year, a junior trader at Société Générale was revealed as having cost the bank a staggering €4.9 billion in unauthorized trading, sending shockwaves throughout the banking system. Thanks to an incredibly lax regulatory environment in Jérôme Kerviel's section of SocGen, he was able to build up a €50 billion exposure to the market, which turned viciously sour and eventually resulted in the crippling ten-figure loss to his bank.

From reading the police report into his actions, Kerviel appears to be the epitome of a binge trader. He was described by colleagues as a *flambeur* (high roller) and a *joueur* (gambler); his rapid addiction to ever-larger trading positions seemed doomed to end in disaster. Whilst he was only employed as an assistant trader, his aptitude for both maths and sweet-talking, combined with an innate compulsion to deceive, meant that he was able to side-step internal compliance procedures and dupe his supervisors into believing that nothing was amiss in his world of complex and fraudulent dealing.

SocGen was the perfect place for someone to get away with such excess: a world leader in equity derivative trading, the banking giant employed almost 150,000 staff around the world, diluting the amount of attention paid to any one area of the business.

After being promoted to the dealing floor from his previous post in the middle office, Kerviel took to the fast-paced, high-octane environment like a duck to water, noted the *New Yorker*. With his higher salary came the pressure of believing he had to prove himself worthy of his pay packet to his colleagues.

'I had realized, during my first meeting in 2005, that I was not as well regarded as the others,' he told police. 'Because I didn't go straight to the front lines – I went through the middle office, and I was the only one that did.' His first mammoth trade came in the summer of 2005, when he sold short of ten million shares in Allianz, banking a fortuitous half a million euros in profit when the 7/7 bombings in London sent the markets lurching downwards.

He described his profitable trade as 'the jackpot', telling of the 'snowball effect' that made him want to continue dealing in that kind of size after such an auspicious start. His bosses' first reaction to his unauthorized, yet profitable, trade was 'satisfaction, naturally', he said, although they cautioned him against taking such huge positions in future.

He didn't heed their advice, risking more and more of the firm's money as his confidence – and lack of restraint – grew. By March 2007 he had open positions totalling almost a billion euros on the German DAX market alone, and by the end of the month his total exposure was €5.6 billion. However, the market was swinging against him in a major way, but he held his nerve and eventually made back the €2.5 billion that he had earlier been losing.

His brother, to whom he'd confided his deeds, begged

him to stop, but he carried on regardless, buoyed in no small part by his growing reputation amongst his trading-room peers.

'Almost every day I was declaring mind-boggling results,' he said, earning him the nickname 'cash machine' at the firm. 'Everyone was super-happy, because we were blowing right through the ceiling,' he recalled, according to the *New Yorker*.

After making €43 million in profit over the course of the year, he received a €300,000 bonus and was amazed that no one at the bank was reining him in and preventing him putting the firm at such risk on a daily basis.

'I thought it was incredible that no one came to talk to me about this. My positions made money, so I told myself that it legitimized what I was doing.'

However, the long arm of the compliance department was, albeit belatedly, catching up with him, and he was soon under intense scrutiny for the gargantuan trading he was undertaking. A SocGen trader had killed himself a year previously, allegedly after unauthorized trading positions were uncovered, so Kerviel was treated with kid gloves by those probing his own misbehaviour.

However, despite all his bluster and his attempts to throw his bosses off the scent, it eventually came to light that he was now sitting on a loss of €1.5 billion, thanks to a badly performing €50 billion trade he was running. Due to the size of the open position, SocGen could not close it all out at once, taking three days to eventually unwind the deal, by which time the losses had more than tripled to just under €5 billion.

Confronted with his misdemeanours, he admitted to trading 'outside the limits of my mandate, which I masked by a fictitious transaction'. He maintained that his primary motivation was 'to make money for the bank', a statement seemingly backed up by the lack of evidence that he had either stolen any money or enjoyed anything like a high-flying life outside the office. He lived in a modest one-bedroom flat and didn't even own a car, let alone any of the other standard baubles that millionaire financiers like to amass.

Kerviel's actions earned him sympathy in some quarters, with many French citizens seeing him as a victim of a profit-obsessed bank. In a poll for *Le Figaro* the week after SocGen announced the Kerviel-caused loss, only 13 per cent of respondents blamed Kerviel for the situation, whereas 59 per cent blamed SocGen itself.

No such compassion appears forthcoming for Bernard Madoff, whose alleged fraud dwarfs even the colossal losses racked up by Kerviel. Madoff, by his own admission, swindled some $50 billion out of those investing in his company, including several major banks, charitable institutions and private individuals.

On 11 December 2008, Madoff was arrested by FBI agents, following a tip-off from his sons that he was running a giant Ponzi scheme: in essence, an enormous pyramid scheme that required a constant inflow of new money in order to pay returns to earlier investors. His firm had been operating in such a fashion for years, producing steady double-digit yields on investors' money, regardless of market conditions (which in itself raised eyebrows among many sceptical observers). However, the scale of the unfolding credit crisis prompted many of his investors to seek to redeem their money from Madoff's fund, precipitating the collapse of his scheme, which was essentially built out of thin air.

Clients wanted to withdraw $7 billion from the firm,

and Madoff was struggling to raise $7 billion to cover redemptions: with more money flowing out than in, there was no way to perpetuate the fraud any longer. On 10 December he suggested to his sons that the firm pay out several million dollars in bonuses two months ahead of schedule, from the $200 million in assets that the firm still had. Then, at his apartment, he admitted to his sons that his firm was a fraud. They confronted their father, asking him how the firm could pay bonuses if it could not pay investors, prompting Madoff's admission that he was 'finished' – after which they promptly reported him to the authorities

The full ramifications of his actions are still unknown, although the immediate impact included the closure of several high-profile charitable trusts with money tied up in Madoff's firm. Several banks, including Banco Santander (owner of Britain's Abbey National building society), revealed that they were heavily exposed to the scam – Santander reckoning its own losses to be close to $3 billion. The SEC, America's financial regulator, announced it would be investigating apparent lapses within its own organization, since allegations began surfacing that Madoff's company had been 'red-flagged' for years by suspicious outsiders, yet the SEC had taken no action to investigate the claims.

It seems that Madoff had pulled the wool over investors' eyes using a staggering level of deception, including denying clients access to electronic records of their investments, instead sending out only printed statements of their accounts. His methods of investment were also called into doubt, with some analysts performing due diligence on Madoff raising alarms because they were unable to replicate the fund's past returns using historic price data for US stocks and options on the indexes.

Rival fund managers were also not able to replicate the same returns, using the strategies from Madoff's quarterly reports.

Madoff had a very successful track record, with returns that were said to be 'unusually consistent'. His returns of around 10 per cent were a key factor in the perpetuation of Madoff's saga for decades; other Ponzi schemes that paid out returns of 20 per cent or higher typically collapsed much faster. A hedge fund run by Madoff, which described its strategy as focused on shares in the S&P 100 index, averaged a 10.5 per cent annual return over the previous seventeen years. Throughout November 2008, amid a general market collapse, the fund reported that it was up 5.6 per cent year-to-date, while the year-to-date total return on the S&P 500 index had been down 38 per cent. One investor in Madoff's fund commented that 'The returns were just amazing, and we trusted this guy for decades. If you wanted to take money out, you always got your cheque in a few days. That's why we were all so stunned.'

Charles Gradante, co-founder of hedge-fund research firm Hennessee Group, observed that Madoff 'only had five down months since 1996', and commented on Madoff's investment performance: 'You can't go ten or fifteen years with only three or four down months. It's just impossible.' A 2001 story in *MARHedge* interviewed traders who questioned how Madoff could have seventy-two gaining months in a row, saying that type of stock success had never occurred before.

Among the other suspicious signs was the fact that Madoff's company avoided filing disclosures of its holdings with the SEC by selling its holdings for cash at the end of each accounting period, a highly unusual tactic.

Madoff's use of a small auditing firm, which had only one active accountant, was also a suspicious move, and was noted by hedge-fund advisory firm Aksia LLC when it advised its clients in 2007 not to invest with Madoff. Furthermore, while hedge funds typically hold their portfolio at a securities firm that acts as the fund's prime broker (usually a major bank or brokerage), allowing an outside investigator to verify their holdings, Madoff's firm was its own broker-dealer and supposedly processed all its own trades.

Less than a fortnight after Madoff's arrest, one of the founders of Access International Advisors LLC, René-Thierry Magon de la Villehuchet, was found dead in his company office on Madison Avenue in New York City. Both of his wrists were slit, and de la Villehuchet had taken sleeping pills. Access International Advisors LLC had invested US$1.4 billion with Madoff's firm, and de la Villehuchet had also invested his personal money with Madoff's business. No suicide note was found at the scene. The FBI and SEC do not believe de la Villehuchet was involved in the fraud – however, there is a strong suspicion that Madoff could not have pulled off a heist of such a vast scale unassisted, and the hunt continues for others who may have helped him in his criminal pursuits.

Madoff's fraud rounded off a sorry year for the world of finance, which had already been left reeling after several high-profile collapses in the banking world. In March 2008 investment bank Bear Stearns buckled under the weight of its losses from the sub-prime mortgage market collapse, resulting in the bank's acquisition at firesale prices by rival JP Morgan. Bear Stearns was sold for $10 per share, a fraction of the $133 price at which the stock had been trading during the previous year, reflecting the severity of the crisis hitting some of the world's banking titans.

Later in the year, Lehman Brothers was driven to file for bankruptcy protection in similar circumstances, sending shockwaves throughout the global financial system. Like Bear Steans, Lehman Brothers was unable to cope with the scale of the fallout from the collapsing sub-prime market, and the company entered into a year-long downward spiral, culminating in its eventual demise.

In August 2007, the firm closed its sub-prime lender, BNC Mortgage, taking an after-tax charge of $25 million and a $27 million reduction in goodwill. The bank said that poor market conditions in the mortgage space 'necessitated a substantial reduction in its resources and capacity in the sub-prime space'. Then, during 2008, Lehman faced an unprecedented loss to the continuing sub-prime mortgage crisis; huge losses accrued in lower-rated mortgage-backed securities throughout 2008. In the second fiscal quarter, Lehman reported losses of $2.8 billion and was forced to sell off $6 billion in assets. In the first half of 2008 alone, Lehman stock lost 73 per cent of its value as the credit market continued to tighten.

Investor confidence continued to erode as Lehman's stock lost roughly half its value and pushed the S&P 500 down 3.4 per cent on 9 September. The Dow Jones lost 300 points the same day on investors' concerns about the security of the bank. The next day, Lehman announced a loss of $3.9 billion and their intent to sell off a majority stake in their investment-management business, which included the firm Neuberger Berman. Lehman, after earlier rejecting questions on the sale of the company, was reportedly searching for a buyer as its stock price dropped another 40 per cent on 11 September 2008.

Just before the collapse of Lehman Brothers, executives at Neuberger Berman allegedly sent e-mail memos suggesting, among other things, that Lehman Brothers' top executives forgo multi-million-dollar bonuses to 'send a strong message to both employees and investors that management is not shirking accountability for recent performance'.

Lehman Brothers' Investment Management Director, George Herbert Walker IV, dismissed the proposal, going so far as to actually apologize to other members of the Lehman Brothers executive committee for the idea of bonus reduction having been suggested: 'Sorry team. I am not sure what's in the water at Neuberger Berman. I'm embarrassed and I apologize.'

On 13 September the president of the Federal Reserve Bank of New York called a meeting on the future of Lehman, which included the possibility of an emergency liquidation of its assets. Lehman reported that it had been in talks with Bank of America and Barclays over the company's possible sale. However, both Barclays and Bank of America ultimately declined to purchase Lehmans in its entirety.

The crisis of confidence caused by Lehmans' impending collapse became so severe that the International Swaps and Derivatives Association offered an exceptional trading session on Sunday 14 September to allow market participants to offset positions in various derivatives on the condition of a Lehman bankruptcy later that day. In New York, shortly before 1 a.m. the next morning, Lehman Brothers Holdings announced it would file for bankruptcy protection, citing bank debt of $613 billion,

$155 billion in bond debt, and assets worth only $639 billion.

Immediately following the bankruptcy filing, an already unstable market began an uncontrollable tailspin. What resulted was what many have called the 'perfect storm' of economic distress factors, and eventually led to a $700 billion bailout package being approved by Congress. The overall erosion of confidence in the banking system – felt by both private individuals as well as banks (who grew fearful of lending to one another in case of further bankruptcies) – continues to grip the markets in a stranglehold, long after Lehman Brothers finally bit the dust.

In the aftermath of 2008's various disasters, fingers have been pointed at the lack of internal controls put in place by various banks, as well as the regulators supposedly overseeing the market players and checking that they act in an orderly and proper fashion in the course of their activities. Alongside the hand-wringing that has ensued both inside and outside the financial communities, much has been made of the supposedly cavalier attitude with which entire corporations treated their business models, all the way from the lowliest traders and brokers to the highest executive officers.

With hindsight it proved easy to highlight the dangers of such reckless investing, but – as Daniel Barnes noted earlier – the atmosphere of the bull market meant that those swept up in the frenzy were encouraged to take risks not only by their superiors, but by the public as well, who urged them on to produce ever-dizzier levels of returns on their behalf.

Looking back, Jerome Kerviel, for one, said he accepted his share of responsibility, 'but it must be acknowledged I was not acting alone. My superiors were indulgent towards my activities. When you're used to making €500,000 every day, at some point it becomes normal. The results, the numbers, become banal,' he continued, echoing the words of David Kyte over twenty years earlier, whose talk of money simply being a way to keep score conjured up images of a trader for whom futures dealing was no different from trying to get the top score on the Space Invaders machine at his local chip shop.

'You're happy,' Kerviel continued, 'but it has less of an effect on you. It's not an ego thing. There are people in the company who are far more brilliant than I am. I was one of the most discreet about results. Truly, my goal was just to increase activity.'

With that explanation, one of the most notorious figures in market mythology sums up, both succinctly and scarily, quite how addictive trading was, is, and will continue to be for generations.

10 Back to the Futures

Broker Steven Gold vehemently opposes the idea that trading is an unsavoury way to make a living.

'The market's not an evil and gambling is not an evil. Gambling is a legitimate thing like smoking is legitimate. Drinking is legitimate. No one's told me by law you can't go and gamble. In terms of morals I don't have any issues with working in the City itself.'

Why do other people harbour such caustic views towards the world of finance?

'I think it's jealousy,' he replies. 'Pure jealousy. They're jealous of people earning more money than them. Having a better lifestyle. There may be 1 or 2 per cent of this population that actually really deep down have a fear and a hatred of people earning money. You know, your real left-wing communists or Socialist Worker types who actually believe that. But I reckon some 99 per cent of the population would swap their job for mine if they could earn that sort of money.

'And there's another thing: how much tax do you think I pay a year? What I contribute to the British economy in income tax is huge. Every month I get my pay cheque and I look at what I pay in tax, and I think that there's people out there that are not working. They're living off benefits, scrounging. They could go out there and do something but they're better off not working, [especially] if they've got a couple of kids. If people have got an issue with me earning decent money then they should be looking at the tax I pay.

'The City is adding wealth to the world in loads of ways. There's a trickle-down effect through the economy. We've got people that deliver newspapers, people that clean the plants, people that clean the floors, people that clean the crap out of the toilets. You know, these African guys that come in twice a day. If we weren't here, they wouldn't have a job. Go down to the sandwich shop next door. That employs fifteen people. It's the knock-on. Not everyone can do the trading jobs. There are receptionists, secretaries, drivers, IT, cleaners – they all have a job because I'm earning commission. If I didn't earn commission and if I didn't do well for my clients, the toilet cleaner wouldn't have a job, because we'd be out of business and there'd be no one on this floor.'

Rob Davis takes a similar view from his West End vantage point.

'Every hedge fund's cutting costs at the moment,' which will impact on the wider workforce too, he warns. 'We had a shoeshine man, we had a three-course lunch delivered every day, we had massages three times a week – they've suspended all of those. So just think, the massage alone was a 100-grand-a-year contract, and if we're doing it, other firms are doing it, so [the massage company] will go out of business. The shoeshine guy, probably on twenty grand a year – finished. Meals that we're not buying off restaurants like Wagamama and Carluccio's – they're going to lose nice business as well. We need the City to make things go round. I've got a mate in the drinks trade, he supplies a lot of the bars round here, and he's struggling. That's the way it goes.'

Gold points out that trickle-down economics does not just stem from those working in the City, but from the clients they service.

'If you create wealth for someone, they'll go and spend that on things,' he explains. 'Say you deal for someone over years, and they take fifty grand out of their portfolio to build an extension on their house. Well, that's going to help the local builder and the local plumber and the local bathroom man, and the local surveyor – so no, I don't have a problem with [the role I play in the system]. Creating more wealth for someone by doing something with their portfolio, and then they go and use that money to buy something – that's a good thing.'

I ask him if the end justifies the means, in that case: does he think working simply to make rich people richer is therefore a good thing?

'If I don't do it someone else will. There'll always be people to do these jobs. To be honest with you, there are very few people in this world that, if you tell them, "If you do this and you do that, then you earn more money," they would say no. More than 99 per cent of people – certainly in this country or the Western world – if you gave them a chance to work in the City, earn good money, they'd bite your hand off.'

Belief that outsiders are jealous of those in the City is common. Darren Carver says that it's all a matter of perception: if people choose to focus on the negative side of the City, then there's little anyone can do to convince them otherwise.

'I would be inclined to agree that it's jealousy fuelling the resentment,' he remarks. 'But it depends how many people are out there flaunting their wealth, doesn't it? There's flaunting your wealth or there's putting it to some

good, isn't there? And the putting it to some good generally goes unreported because people can't see it, because
all people can see is the gleaming red Ferrari.

'There's such a cynical view towards the City. There's
a lot of charity going on behind the scenes that goes
unreported, but the good stuff doesn't really sell newspapers, does it? They set us up high and kick us when
we're down. But no one really points out how much
income these firms actually generate in terms of tax rev-
enue and so on. There are two sides to every story, and
who's actually out there speaking on behalf of the City?'

Some traders believe that the public's coolness towards
the City stems from their lack of understanding of what
goes on within the world of finance: the principle that
'one fears what one doesn't understand'. Others, including Paul O'Connor, have encountered the polar opposite point of view.

'I've never found people saying, "I don't understand it,
I hate it." My experience is, "I don't understand it, I'm
fascinated by it." I think that people, the public, society
are fascinated by wealth, aren't they? And the fact that
there are these huge amounts of money being made and
traded and banked by people fascinates the public.

'Our society has always been fascinated by wealth; if
you look at art, literature, a hell of a lot of the inspiration
for art and literature is wealth. I mean my partner and his
artist friends, who've never worked in finance or had
anything to do with it, are fascinated by it. They always
used to ask me questions about it, and I used to think, it's
fucking boring, why are you asking me questions about
this? You're in a much more interesting field. But they
used to be constantly intrigued, because they didn't
understand it. There's a smoke and mirrors aspect to the

markets and financial companies that fascinates people, because they think it's so confusing and rocket science-like – which, by the way, it's not.'

Damien Walsh, on the other hand, is typically outspoken when it comes to the public's relationship with financiers, arguing that a combination of ignorance and envy fuels society's rage against the City machine.

'Generally people don't understand what I do, including my friends, who I've explained it to twenty times. These are smart people, and if they don't understand it, I don't expect Joe Public to understand it. And again the resentment has to be about the money. So, for example, a sales team are going to resent their manager for not having to sit on the phones all day like they are while he's raking in the cash. It's the same with anything. In any industry. What do they resent? Do they resent that the City makes the world go round? Do they resent the fact that the City enables most of the industry that they work in?

'It's all about money, that's the funny thing. The irony is that everyone's bitter about these people that make so much money. What is it about them they don't like? Is it because they drink wine in suits? I just don't know what it is, except for the fact they earn more money. Is it because they don't work hard? Because they fucking do. People think traders don't have any stress, but believe me they do – I'm sure that there must be a higher rate of anxiety and depression amongst traders than in any other industry. Broking is the closest thing to trading, and even brokers can't really understand what it's like to be a trader. Trading's still so far removed, because your whole everything is on the line all the time, and it's not your client you're fucking up for, it's the big pile of money that was part yours, which is now a quarter of the size because you've fucked up. Again.'

He sees the City as an inevitable manifestation of the greed ethos in which society at large has been gripped for years.

'It's the rise of the bling culture, and it's a by-product of people being wealthy and people searching for money. Greed is seen as such a dirty word, because it's one of the seven deadly sins, but it propels everyone in every walk of life. Even the charity sector. There are five main charities in this country, and they compete with each other constantly; because they're charities they can't do it actively, but they are basically at each other's throats. Everything's competitive and, unfortunately, it's been decided that capitalism is the way for the world to grow. Everyone needs to make money.'

What about people for whom making money is a secondary goal, who put first issues such as working to better the lot of those worse off than them?

'I know it's hard for people in the charity sector. I do think the charity sector is underpaid. But we live in a world that is judged by financial indicators, and we know that your success is judged by how much money you've got – as such, the people that earn the most money have to be doing the hardest jobs. If you want to earn the most money, go and do that job. Why aren't you doing that job? Is it because you can't? Yes – obviously. Otherwise why wouldn't you do it? Or is it because you want to give something to the world? Great! But that doesn't pay much money.

'I'm really glad there are people that put things above money, but they're in the minority. I do agree that it feels unfair that so few people should earn so much money, but it's the nature of the world. The alternatives have been tried as well, and if a few rich people are the downside to free trade and the ability of people to make money from the ground up, I'll deal with that. But I think maybe that's an understanding that I've got from being a trader.'

He believes it is blinkered to single out the City as the only arena which people enter seeking money as a primary goal.

'Why does anyone do anything? I mean, I don't think most people become lawyers because they think they can be Erin fucking Brockovich taking on BP. I don't think doctors think they're going to be George Clooney. You see these fucking guys with their superfoods and their fucking organic nuts and whatever, and they're like, "I'm doing this because it's all about Mother Nature . . ." No you're not. You're doing it to go to the next festival and drop a load of acid, for fuck's sake. You're doing it so you can enjoy the life that you want to lead, as self-righteous as it is. At least in finance you have honesty. Really, is anyone trying to do anything but feed their family?

'Trading is a risky industry to go into. Say you go into charity work: by the time you're forty years old you'll be earning fifty grand a year. You'll be on your way to executive level. You're going to be very employable until you're sixty, at which point they'll stick you in some fucking room and give you a watch. But in trading, you can be out in two years. You can be out in three days with literally nothing.

'If anyone can tell me that that's a risk that they're comfortable taking, then they're probably a trader. And those who aren't are bitter that they're not, and I think that's where a lot of the resentment from the public comes in. Because it is a huge leap of faith in yourself, and most people don't have that.'

I ask him to clarify an earlier point: was he referring to simply the people who manufacture 'superfoods', or those who consume their products?

'The people that produce them. But people that eat them are cunts as well, don't get me wrong . . .' he replies, lighting another cigarette and leaning back on his sofa, a half-smile, half-scowl playing across his lips.

James Blackburn of Execution Ltd takes a similar view to Damien, in terms of pointing out society's willing acceptance of capitalism as the model of choice in the modern era.

'Capitalism's what we have, it's what the world does, it's what makes the world go round. Has there been greed and avarice in the City over the last five years, exceptional greed and exceptional avarice? Yes, there has. Not necessarily more than in other walks of life, but the City is the focal point from which other stuff is spread out.'

He does not believe that those within the City are divorced from reality, nor that they don't appreciate the effect the latest downturn is having on the rest of society.

'I think people in the City know exactly what the man on the street is going through, because I think there have been probably more job losses in the City on a relative basis. You read every day about thousands and thousands of job losses, and I don't care whether you're earning fifty grand or you're earning 300 grand. If you earn fifty grand and you lose your job, you had a fifty-grand lifestyle, and life becomes very difficult. When you have 300 grand, and you lose your job, you had a 300-grand lifestyle and now you've got nothing. The City isn't immune to the pain; it feels it acutely. I don't think

I'm in a City bubble. We absolutely know we're very fortunate.'

As James points out, the aftermath of the credit crunch is at the forefront of the minds of everyone in the City, just as it is in the rest of society. However, the way in which the press has pilloried the Square Mile and hung its workers out to dry for apparently being solely responsible for the crisis has angered many.

Daniel Barnes blames the press for the climate of hate towards bankers and traders, a stance he thinks they've taken 'because they don't understand it. Honestly, they have no fucking clue.' Are the press bowing to public demand for a City target on whom to pin all the blame, or are they creating the scapegoats themselves and encouraging their readers to think the same way?

'I think it's both. I think whenever anything goes wrong people want a scapegoat. It's a very impulsive and instinctive reaction of human beings, but what scapegoating does is hide a much darker reality.

'I think when people want to know the truth – if they ever do – they'll realize that it's not about a few people who went haywire. It's about people who collectively accepted a system that allowed everyone to behave in such a way that created the mess that we're in. Quite frankly neither the press nor their readers really know, so both parties are trying to scapegoat. It makes for much better reading, but I think the press have a greater responsibility to relay the right message.'

Damien Walsh is similarly strident in his attack on the press for what he feels is a clear-cut case of double standards.

'Scapegoat is the right word, because scapegoats are most often the things that people don't understand, and no one that isn't in finance understands finance – mostly because they haven't taken the time to learn about it. It's a reflexive action of hating things that you don't understand. And it's typified by the short-selling ban – a short-sighted move that obviously wasn't going to have any tangible effect. All it did was protect a handful of government friends for no long-term gain.'

On this point, I am in complete agreement, I tell him. I wrote several pieces for the *Guardian* on the subject of the nonsensical outlawing of short-selling, which was hastily dropped by the government in early 2009. My opinions saw me hauled across the coals by readers who left furious comments on the *Guardian*'s website, despite having little to no idea what short-selling really was. Instead, their knee-jerk castigation of anyone engaging in the practice was revealing: many people suspend reason in times of crisis and scramble aboard the nearest bandwagon as a way of assuaging their uncertainty.

'The ban made people feel the government was doing something,' continues Walsh. 'That they didn't need to panic just yet. And all it did was delay the panic. All it did was make people feel self-righteous about the fact that financiers were bad people because they sold short of stock. I mean they invented a group of people that doesn't even exist.'

I suggest that short-sellers, and subsequently traders in general, are being cast in unwarranted roles as pantomime villains, but he takes it one step further. 'They're not being painted as pantomime villains,' he says. 'They're being painted as genuine, grassroots scapegoats. It's complete bigotry and ignorance.

'You look at the oil industry, the diamond industry, whatever – they all get away with fucking murder,' he rants. 'With someone that works in a biological or chemical company, or an oil company, you can very easily say that they are fucking people over. But it's hard to say that a trader is fucking someone over. If anything, it's the banks doing it, because they're the only people that have the kind of money to do that. With a trader, he's being told what to do. They're not consulted, and they don't say, "Oh, we're going to start doing credit default swaps, what do you think?" They just get told, this is what we're doing now – trade it. Bang. Here's the market, get going.'

In Walsh's view, the recent collapse should not provoke across-the-board regulatory restrictions on the markets. Only the areas at fault for the present situation should be tackled.

'The only thing that should be restricted is the over-the-counter shit that only the funds and the banks get to trade, because that's the deregulated stuff. Any futures, CFDs, normal fair equities, they're all already so regulated to the hilt that you can't do anything wrong. You can't even trade a single share beyond your limit. Whereas this other stuff is done with closed books. No one gets to see it, and that's where holes appear. All these massive credit swaps and debt swaps.

'Why do you think it's gone wrong? Because no one knows what they're worth, because all you're doing is saying to your mate, "Hook me up. We'll both call it this on our books, and then we're sweet as." Most traders aren't them. Most traders are like me. That's the numbers of it, but we get the flak. It's definitely a financial problem, but it's a financial problem at a high level. Traders are seen as being this omni–potent force, and it's so far from the truth. The people that really screw anyone over are the people at the top.'

However, he holds out little hope of others coming

round to his way of thinking; at least, he says, not while the media continue to offer jaundiced and ill-informed views of the markets.

'The misunderstanding of trading is typified every day in newspapers by fucking photos that show elated traders when the market's had a good day, and pissed-off traders when the market's had a bad day. Like that couldn't change ten seconds later, or like that couldn't have been from a different day when the market was doing the opposite. It's a fallacy that markets up is necessarily good, and that markets down is necessarily bad. Everything's interrelated, so a certain [stock] going up when nothing else is going up can be a bad sign.'

Uncomprehending outside observers are one of Rob Davis's pet hates.

'People who have a go at hedge funds? Well, they don't even know what they're talking about,' he says angrily. 'Look at the situation [with short-selling being banned in banking stocks]. Bottom line is, the banks were going bust, so the hedge funds were right. Everyone says it's market manipulation, but it's not – that was the right price for the shares. If it weren't for the hedge funds, the banks would still have problems, and the problems would be coming out now. The hedge funds only accelerated the process. These banks were going bust, unless the government saved them. So ultimately the hedge funds were right. People criticizing us were not thinking logically. The easiest people to blame are the hedge funds.'

Yet Jeremy Lyon, despite having spent his entire working career in the City, has no problem taking aim at hedge funds.

'They're spivs', he declares. 'I haven't got much respect for them, honestly – they're loose cannons.'

He blames the new-school lust for fast profits at any cost as one of the reasons the City's image has been so tarnished of late.

'The impression of a stockbroker has definitely gone downhill. If you're in the finance department of a broking firm you're divorced from the business. Whereas the person on the sales desk with the telephone and the screen, he is the spiv.'

Lyon, who earlier praised the market of yesteryear as being almost military in its code of conduct, believes that seemingly small matters such as rules of appearance have a big influence on how those within the City treat their work.

'One's personal behaviour is part of one's standing, and that's where broking has gone downhill. It was the same at Lehman [Brothers]: they all liked having their Friday off, and their standards dropped and they became desperate for business, and that's sad. I'm hoping that'll change again, that the impression of a stockbroker becomes that he is a gentle and honest and straight professional.'

Michael Parnes believes the image of the City will take a turn for the better, despite the ill-will.

'I think the public will look at the City in a new light, because it's a new era, it's a time where the stereotype of the yuppie and the big bonuses are going to be reduced quite a bit. On the back of this crisis the papers have made out it's all because of the City, and people being paid bonuses and fees for arranging credit. For coming up with these complicated financial structures like CDOs which have all collapsed and created difficult unwinding situations for working out who owes what. As well as the fact that there's no end user: we've been repackaging debt in complex manners, selling it without anyone to pay for it at the end of the day, and it's now unravelling before our very eyes.

'That is why City boys have been demonized, and quite rightly so: greed. However, I think in time we're not going to be motivated like that; things will be straight and simple and clear, and the City will have a better name in the future. It's been necessary for this to happen, but things will clear themselves up, and the City will look better, because this won't happen again, this greed.'

City lawyer Miles Clarke (not his real name) is similarly understanding of the public's current antipathy towards bankers.

'People are entitled to be angry and upset when the system ceases to work, and when it does so in a way which some people foresaw. But you can't blame people for doing their job. They carry out their jobs within set parameters.

'The structural error was the reward system in the City. The reward system meant that both the institutions and individuals were never in a position where they personally paid the price for things going wrong. If things went wrong, then the government would come in and bail out the institution, and if you were very unlucky, you might lose your job. But at a personal level, if you have a bonus culture where people get bonuses which are huge irrespective of whether they are performing well, whether they've made disastrous decisions or not, then all the impetus is in maximizing that short-term profit, knowing that you will never be in a position where you will have to carry the can.'

Clarke says it will prove a daunting task to convince the public to trust the City once more.

'Public confidence in financial institutions will have taken a huge knock, and it will take a long time for trust to flood back in. But these things have happened before: public confidence in markets took a huge knock when the dot-com bubble burst, and at the end of the day there are people who need to save money for their retirement and will put money into pension funds. And pension funds will continue to invest in securities, so things will eventually come back.'

He also doesn't fault the public for resenting the vast salaries some brokers and traders take home, 'because it seems to be unearned, and people have a clear sense that there are jobs that are worth doing and jobs that are not worth doing. So a teacher or nurse is greatly socially valued, whereas estate agents, lawyers and journalists have always been the whipping boys. Bankers have more or less got away with it, but now they are going to be whipping boys as well. I don't think opprobrium is wholly unearned in all cases.'

However, he is not prepared to tar the entire banking industry with the same, condemnatory brush.

'What I do is I tell financial sector agencies who are desperate to get it right what they need to do in order to avoid breaching the regulatory rules. And financial institutions are filled with people who are absolutely desperate to be doing things correctly, and to be seen to be doing things correctly.

'The question that really arises then is, does the system that governs them place the right expectations on them? That works at two levels. First of all, are the FSA's rules and the legislation that governs the regulation of financial services put together in the right way? Is it missing the point? Is it failing because it's structured the wrong way? Secondly – and more importantly – what is the compliance culture in a particular institution? I can't name names, but there are some institutions where the internal structure of decision-making puts complying with regulation very much at the heart of what goes on, and in other institutions it's dealt with in a very haphazard way. It's the institutions which have not got the structure right which have most egregiously breached regulatory rules.'

He maintains that the FSA are stepping up their efforts to combat fraud and abuse in the markets.

'The FSA has really beefed up its monitoring software,' he tells me. 'There was a big shift from insider-dealing prosecutions – which were very difficult and very, very expensive to bring: you needed the absolute clearest of evidence – to the market-abuse regime which came in 2001. The FSA is doing more investigations into market abuse, and the regime was also beefed up in 2005 as well with the European Market Abuse Directive, which placed strong procedural requirements on firms to ensure that all the evidence was available to the FSA when they came in to ask questions.

'The FSA does now ask difficult questions, and act on it as well. I have had clients whose careers in the City have come to an end because they engaged in market abuse. These are people who went from the very top of their careers in major financial institutions to basically twiddling their thumbs at home with nothing. I had a client who burst into tears in the middle of a meeting because the FSA were obviously going to say, "Sorry, mate, that's the end of your career." Perhaps not for ever – the FSA do consider that you can be a re-habilitated market abuser – but you're never going to get back to where you were. I think the problems that we have at the moment are about financial institutions doing the equivalent of going to work in shorts and

Bermuda shirts because they believed it was never going to rain.'

Clarke cautions against rash government intervention into the markets.

'You want to make sure that you're not destroying a socially useful industry,' he says. 'A lot of what I do, a lot of what people in the City do, is facilitate pension funds in getting a sufficient number of assets into their funds, in order to pay the old age pensions of elderly people. One of the things I do is talk to pension fund managers from all over the world who are absolutely desperate to make sure that old people don't die in penury, and the way they do this is by investing in the markets. Doing it by private equity funds and hedge funds or CDO funds, buying chunks of financial institutions when they're at rock bottom in the hope that they'll be worth more in the future.'

Is that really what he thinks drives these fund managers, I ask – desperation to make sure that pensioners don't lose out?

'Well, it is where a huge share of the money comes from,' he replies. 'There are some places – in Singapore, for example – where some of the sovereign wealth funds have so much money and such a great need to maximize the return on their investment, because if they don't, old people will starve. If we lived in small rural communities, our grandparents would be living with us. We'd go out to work and we'd feed them, but the way we do this in a large globalized economy is that old people invest in private pensions, or they have money invested in company pensions, or they live in a country like Singapore where money is deducted at source and goes into the pension fund. That money is put away and invested for their old age. It is people who are coming up for retirement now who are the primary victims of what's happening in the City at the moment.'

The pensioner-friendly, unfairly maligned City that the likes of Clarke describe is, of course, light years away from the malicious entity perceived by certain quarters of the public. The sense of schadenfreude emanating from commentators of late is reminiscent of the post-Black Monday mood in late 1980s Britain. Back then, Simon Jenkins gloated from the sidelines that 'the yuppies had it coming to them! Now let's watch them pawn their Porsches, drown in their champagne, rot in their second homes. Thanks goodness the monstrous horde had only a year of glory before its demise.'

Today's columnists are no less vituperative in their anti-City rhetoric, with one of the most notorious examples of the current media witchhunt found in the pages of the *Daily Mirror*. There, a photograph of hedge-fund manager Philip Falcone – 'whose greed has helped bring HBOS to its knees' – was accompanied by a hysterical headline that apparently summed up the mood of a nation: 'GREEDY PIG,' it screamed.

Marina Hyde, writing in the *Guardian*, ended a sneering tirade against bankers with the pay-off: 'Perhaps senior bankers could be required to wander up and down high streets wearing boards reading something along the lines of: "My industry isn't very good at its job and now you might lose your house. I. Am. Sorry."'

The baying for blood continues, with financiers making the leap from theoretical pantomime villains to actual ones in Christmas 2008 shows. Comedians incorporate anti-City jokes into their acts (although not all comics were so quick to throw stones from their glass houses, Andy Zaltzman pointing out that 'We can't really complain about capitalism backfiring on us like this. As my grandmother used to say: "There's no point whinging about being eaten by a horse if you've decided to play polo dressed as a sugar lump . . .'")

From looking into the gulf between those on either side of the City barricades, it's clear that there is no likely imminent rapprochement. As long as we refuse to see the City as a monster of society's creation – one which admittedly condenses some of humanity's worst traits and thrives on their exploitation – there is no chance of getting to grips with the core malaise. Similarly, whilst those in the City continue to adopt a Millwall FC-style attitude of 'no one likes us, we don't care,' there is no incentive for them to heed the advice and demands of the public, whom those in the Square Mile prefer to dismiss as intemperate ignoramuses.

The last word on the subject ought to go to Damien Walsh, who – despite his at-times rabid attacks on anyone outside the trading-room bear pit – actually sums up the City/public stand-off best.

'I'm sorry that Communism didn't work. I was well up for it. I love sharing. But it doesn't seem practical, and as such I don't understand why anyone would think that the City's any worse than the rest of the country. I don't even see that side of the City as an addiction per se, I see it as human nature. Everyone needs to make money.'

Postscript:
First They Came for the Financiers . . .

From archbishops to arch-socialists, from tabloid editors to the outraged man on the street, there is a belief that, if you trade stocks for a living, you are inherently corrupt and out to destroy the fabric of society. This school of thought has had a surge in disciples of late, as the dust settles in the aftermath of the credit crisis.

Consider the following outburst from Professor Noreena Hertz: 'Do we really want to live in a society in which those who have gambled with our livelihoods end up driving Porsches, while those who save our lives can't afford the petrol to get to work?'

Granted, the subject of her piece is nurses versus bankers, published in the *Guardian*, rather than a tabloid frenzy about hard-grafting members of the white working class versus asylum-seeking benefit recipients. But that doesn't detract from the rabble-rousing vitriol which screams from the page.

Financial crises bring out the worst in people: scapegoats are the order of the day and seized upon with glee. Castigating the trading community is not on a par with race riots or systematic state persecution, but the common theme is the mob mentality that greases the wheels of the vigilante movement. It is always easier to blame a minority for the majority's ills, rather than look in the mirror and assess whether some of the responsibility lies closer to home.

British society has a schizophrenic approach towards those deemed successful. Footballers, pop stars, artists and authors all find their achievements somewhat of a poisoned chalice when the press and public turn on them. Traders, brokers and bankers are no different in that respect: previously heralded for being at the vanguard of a new dawn when the markets were in bull territory, they now find themselves cast as a public enemy.

During my interview with Jonny White, the Canary Wharf futures trader, he remarked that 'what you're doing with your book is really good for the City . . .' In his eyes, I – as a former insider – was out to prove the City's critics wrong and bring to the surface the kind-hearted benevolence of those within the Square Mile. But that was never my intention: instead I wanted to shine a light on an area that garners enormous attention, yet is little understood.

I've learned that the City (with all its faults) is essentially a manifestation of the wider ills of today's culture of instant gratification and immediate returns. Whether you're looking at drugs, drink, purchasing power, pornography or any of the other myriad 'needs' of modern society, the City is reactive in the wider scheme of things.

Those working in the City are not a different species; at least, they weren't when they began their careers. Eighteen-year-olds are malleable, lured by the golden carrots dangled in front of them by employers keen to wring their best years out of them. They gravitate towards a life in the City out of a sense that their standing in society will receive a huge boost, thanks to the mammon-worshipping culture that exists far beyond the City streets.

Give a man a fish, and he'll eat for a day; teach him to deal December fish futures, and he'll trade like a dervish for a lifetime. Those for whom trading is now second nature have detailed in their interviews how hard it is to kick the habit even once they've realized how soul-destroying such a way of life can be. Whether it's Rob Davis and his muscle spasms, Damien Walsh and his Somme-like descriptions of the trading floor, or even Simon Cawkwell and his frank admission that he is addicted to the markets, the cautionary tales should cause anyone about to dive into the fray to sit back and think long and hard about whether it's a world they really want to enter.

I came, saw, and conquered my own City-based compulsive habits, voting with my feet and putting thousands of miles between me and my former stomping ground. But even as I sit writing in my Jerusalem home, far from the madding crowd and with an entirely new way of life, the Siren's song still plays softly in the back of my mind. All it takes is a quick glimpse of CNBC, or a snatched glance at a market report on Sky News, for the trading itch to start. For those who spend every day in front of banks of monitors, the pull of the trading screen is infinitely stronger, holding them vice-like in its grip.

Those fiddling whilst the economy burns, aiming flamethrowers in the direction of the Square Mile, should reflect on what it is that spurred the markets to morph into the destructive shape they take today. If society chooses capitalism, then the public has to accept that the City is the heart that pumps the blood around the system. They can't complain that the heart beats: beating is what hearts do.

There will, of course, be times when the heart gets a murmur or an irregular rhythm, but that is when a statin should be inserted to regulate it. Is the irregularity really caused by the heart itself or by a strain from another part of the body, due to an unhealthy trait? Until the question is answered, and the subject dealt with in an honest fashion, the phenomenon of binge trading is doomed to continue unchecked, consuming those both inside and outside the City's walls.

Acknowledgements

Thanks to everyone who helped with the research for *Binge Trading*: Coline, Simon, Harry, Jeremy, Roy, Nick, James, Michael and all those who remain safely hidden behind the opaque screen of anonymity.

Thanks to Mum and Dad, Rosa and Andrew, Grandma and Grandpa, Granny and Grandad – all of whom watched with bated breath whilst I served my respective countries in a combination of pinstriped suits and combat boots, and all of whom seem to prefer it in print than in real life.

Thanks to Uncle John for the three-dice theory and NOCD.

Thanks to Uncle Michael for China, Texas and Sunday mornings on the football pitch.

Thanks to Rachel, Nic, Oli, Geord and Josh for defending the indefensible.

Thanks to Justin Sandler, O'H, for showing me the ropes – likewise Lawrence, Lee and Stacey.

Thanks to Jo for allegedly being my muse.

Thanks to Ophir for sorting me out.

Thanks to Joel and Mal for making *Binge Trading* happen at all.

Finally, thanks to everyone who lived through Belvedere Court's darkest days, between summer 2001 and spring 2002: Navah, Lauren, Natalie, Adam and Baz. Somehow, it neither killed us nor made us stronger . . .